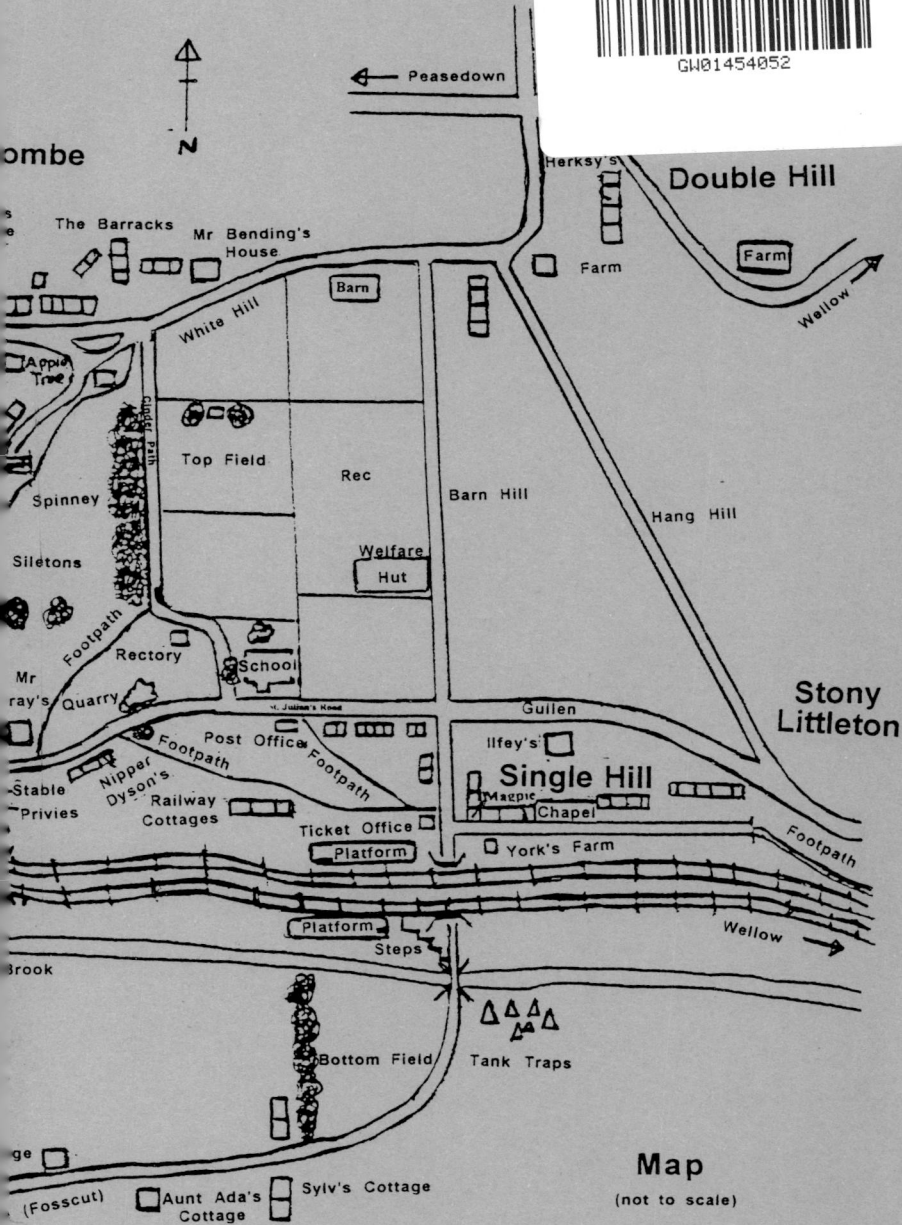

Map

(not to scale)

Pat Armstrong

HAYSEEDS

IN THE

CIDER

PATRICK BOYLE

First published in Great Britain in 1998 by

H.P.B. Books Ltd., 4 Laverton Court,

Edward Street, Westbury, Wilts. BA13 3DP

Title: Hayseeds in the Cider

Author: Patrick Boyle.

Illustrations by: The author and Paul Thomas

ISBN 0 9535625 0 6

Printed and Bound by: H.P.B. Books Ltd., 4 Laverton Court,

Westbury, Wilts. BA13 3DP

HAYSEEDS

IN THE

CIDER

PATRICK BOYLE

First published in Great Britain in 1998 by

H.P.B. Books Ltd., 4 Laverton Court,

Edward Street, Westbury, Wilts. BA13 3DP

Title: Hayseeds in the Cider

Author: Patrick Boyle.

Illustrations by: The author and Paul Thomas

ISBN 0 9535625 0 6

Printed and Bound by: H.P.B. Books Ltd., 4 Laverton Court,

Westbury, Wilts. BA13 3DP

SPECIALLY DEDICATED TO:

THE TREASURED MEMORIES OF MY MOTHER AND MY DEAR FRIEND

FRANK WEST ON

:

ALSO

To the memories of Margaret Weston, Valerie Deverell, Glenda Collins, Vera Young, Ted Horler, Doug Wallace, Jim Swansbury and Jack Weston, all friends of our childhood but who now, sadly, are no longer with us.

ACKNOWLEDGEMENTS

To Mrs Ella Drew, formerly of the Apple Tree, for giving me so much of her time and invaluable assistance with many of the details and anecdotes in the story.

Mr Bob Goode, former Headmaster of St. Julian's School Shoscombe, for making available documents and photographs.

The staffs of the Somerset Guardian at Midsomer Norton, and the Hadyn Coal Museum, for allowing me unlimited access to back copies of their paper.

The staffs of Radstock and Frome libraries, not only for their assistance in providing relevant books, but also for their forebearance.

*Sleeping memories of childhood
hang suspended on the invisible threads of time until,
awakened by a sight or sound or smell, they draw us back
into those far off days of how it used to be.*

ONE

I'll stand on the bridge and wave to you," said mother to my older brother George and me, putting her arms round us and hugging us tightly. Then turning quickly so that we would not see her tears, she walked away from us. We watched her until she was lost to our sight among the milling mass of people, mainly children like ourselves, who filled the platform. All around us other mothers and fathers were sobbing goodbyes to their children before they too made their own lonely journeys back to homes which now would be peopled only with the sounds and memories of many yesterdays.

Many of the children were crying and clinging onto their parents, pleading with them not to go. One boy standing near us begged his mother to stay with him and would have charged after her if a lady wearing a green uniform had not grabbed and held him, struggling and crying, to her.

It was September 3rd 1939, and a day that had begun full of late summer promise had become one of frenzied activity when, a few hours earlier, the Prime Minister had informed the Nation that Great Britain was once again at war with Germany and plans that had been made during the preceding years were now being implemented.

We had just arrived home from church when Mr Bunyan, our next door neighbour, came in and told us the news, adding we were to leave as soon as possible. It was then that all the activity over the preceding weeks, when mother had spent much of her spare time writing our names on pieces of white tape and then sewing them onto each article of our clothing, began to make some kind of sense.

When we had asked her why she was doing it, we were told we might be going away and had to be ready to leave at a moments notice.

"Going away!" "Where?" "When?" "For how long?" Our questions charged at her demanding answers.

"I don't know that myself. All I know is that we have to be ready to leave if we are told to," she explained.

The question of when had now been answered by Mr Bunyan. The answers to where? and for how long? would have to wait until another time.

Less than an hour later, in company with mother, our gas masks hanging from our shoulders and each of us carrying a small suitcase, we left the house and began our journey to the railway station.

Along the way hosts of other children with their mothers and fathers were making the same journey, and whether babies, infants or older children we all had one thing in common ....*identity labels*. Made from luggage tags or pieces of white card that were either pinned to our jackets or hung around the neck on pieces of string, they proclaimed who we were, where we came from and the school, if any, we attended. They also for that moment in time, turned us into one large family with the collective name of 'Evacuee'.

The pavements of the streets along which we walked were packed with people laughing, crying and waving. Many pushed out of the crush to embrace some of the children as we walked past, hugging them as if they would never let them go. Some had to be physically separated.

*   *   *

The scene that greeted our arrival was unbelievable. The entire station was a bedlam of noise and people who all, or so it seemed to me, wanted to stand on the small area of the platform that I was inhabiting. I was pushed, pulled, shoved and jostled; there seemed to be no order or control to the constant movement while at intervals, as if they were being forced unwillingly into the melange of humanity, came the trains, the carriage doors opening to receive their quota of children while the engines gasped their disapproval at such undisciplined behaviour.

Somehow, in the midst of all the noise and the seemingly uncontrollable crush, we had our identity tags and gas masks checked. Those who had arrived without tags had them made for them there on the platform.

It was the fear of gas attacks, similar to those used in the First World War with horrific and deadly effect, that led to everyone, including babies, being issued with a gas mask, that had to be carried at all times. To be caught without it was to incur a severe penalty.

A big problem was the fear those life-saving pieces of apparatus put into many babies, younger children and elderly. That they were, thankfully, never required, was just one of the many unrecorded blessings that wartime Britain enjoyed.

Another drawback was the eyepieces in the face mask which, if they were not cleaned properly with the tube of hard paste provided, tended to steam up, giving the effect of trying to see where you were going on a foggy day.

No-one it appeared knew where we were going. If they did it was being kept a closely guarded secret. The uncertainty that it caused had the effect of forming us into smaller groups within the much larger group.

The group in which we found ourselves differed not at all from the other groups around us with regard to age and range of emotions being paraded. Some of the children were crying, some laughing and fooling around, while others stood quietly with those 'I'm-not-in-the-least-bit-bothered' looks on their faces, while all the time they were as unsure and confused as the rest of us.

As time dragged on an afternoon that had begun on a note of high excitement, with laughter and jokes, singing well-known songs and calling out to the children and parents we knew all making the day seem bright and special, began to sour.

We asked one of the ladies who had checked our gas masks when our train would come.

"Soon," she told us.

We asked where we were going.

"I can't tell you that."

Why not? we wanted to know.

"It's a secret, that's why not," was her reply.

Next we wanted to know why, as some of the children were taking their mothers, we couldn't all take our mothers.

"Because it's a special trip that's mainly for children. Only a few mothers are allowed to go. But you'll be able to tell yours all about it when you see them again.

'When you see them again!'

Five small words to reassure us that it would not be long before we would be back with our parents. Little did any of us know just how long it would be before we saw them again.

The saddest thing of all was the fact that for many of the parents and children there, that day would be the last time they would ever see one another. Bombs, accidents, and plain abandonment would be the main causes.

As many were soon to discover, life is certainly a cruel and mindless beast when it enters into partnership with war, for it is only then that it shows, in infinite ways, the true bestiality of those who perform the marriage ceremony.

*   *   *

I sat down next to George who was sitting with his back to one of the iron pillars supporting the roof and let the tide of movement flow around us. Many of the children on the platform with us that day were as thin, grey-faced and dirty, as the clothes they wore. From questioning eyes set in already old faces that perched precariously on shoulders that were already starting to stoop, they looked out at the world they believed had finally abandoned them.

The saying there is always someone 'worse off' than you was tragically borne out that day. While we were milling around complaining about the long wait for our train to arrive, other mothers and children flailed about in the icy waters of the North Atlantic where two hundred miles off the west coast of Ireland, the liner Athenia had been torpedoed and sunk by a German submarine with the loss of one hundred and twelve lives, of which many were women and children.

Although the suddenness of our leaving had affected us both differently, there were two ways in which George and I felt the same. First was the feeling of great excitement of going to an unknown place, and all the things there would be to see and do there.

The second was one of sadness, for leaving home had also meant leaving our garden, an area where mother hung out the washing and we played our games, chased one another and the butterflies that visited and watched as bees, their tiny legs ballooned to three times their normal size by the pollen that clung to them, searched each flower that mother grew there. There was also a small grassed area where on warm sunny days, we had picnics and read our books. To anyone else it may have been nothing special, but it was to us and we loved it.

Sitting there together we surveyed all the things that we had with us. Our gas masks in their cardboard boxes which were secured to us by a string handle that passed over our head and onto the shoulder so that it hung diagonally across our chest, making it easy to take them out and put on quickly if we had to. Beside them, our suitcases packed with all our newly name-taped clothing and a brown paper carrier bag, one of which each child had been handed after having their name tags and gas masks checked, which contained a tin of soup, a tin of corned beef, a tin of evaporated milk, some sandwiches an apple and a bar of milk chocolate.

A boy of George's age, who told us his name was Jim, came over with his younger sister Daisy and sat down beside us. While they began talking, Daisy and I ate the sandwiches and apples from our bags.

As the waiting trains filled and left with no noticeable reduction in the number of children still on the platform or a lessening in the volume of noise, other trains pulled in to take their place and the exercise would begin again. At last our train arrived and stood waiting for us to board, the huge engine sighing gently, its steam rising like breath on a cold morning, while behind it the carriages welcomed us with open doors.

*   *   *

George and I sat in a corner seat by the window facing the engine as other

4

children came into the compartment. The last person to enter was a teacher named Mrs Farthing who sat in a corner seat by the door leading to the corridor.

The compartment, although full, was quiet and peaceful in comparison to all the noise and bustle of the platform. From other compartments sounds of laughter and the buzz of voices could be heard, punctuated by the sharp rap of feet as other children made their way along the corridor to find seats of their own.

On the seat directly opposite sat Jim and Daisy. Next to them sat two girls aged about eight and four years. The older of the two girls had the most vivid red hair I had ever seen. On the seat beside them sat a boy and girl who looked enough alike to be brother and sister.

The boy on the seat beside us sat in silence clutching his suitcase on his knees, while large tears splashed down onto his hands and ran like small rivers across the surface of the case leaving behind them only dark lines in memory of their passing. Between that boy and the teacher sat another two boys and a girl.

The little girl opposite suddenly began to add her tears to those of the boy. Not in silence like the boy, but in an I-want-the-entire-world-to-know-I'm-crying fashion. Great sobs shook her body, accompanied by shudders and moans.

"What's the matter with her?" George asked the older girl.

"She's upset because they wouldn't let her Danny come as well," explained the girl." She wants to go back home to Danny and her mother."

"Perhaps they'll let her brother come on the next train," volunteered Jim. "Perhaps there wasn't room for him on this one."

"Brother! What do you mean brother?" the red haired girl wanted to know. "Danny's not her brother. She hasn't got any brothers. Danny's her dog. She's only got Danny and her mum. She had a dad but he bunked off with her from up the road."

"Our mother's going to stand up on the bridge and wave to us," I told her. "Isn't she?" I said, looking at George for confirmation of what I said. "Perhaps her mother will be there and have Danny with her."

It was a suggestion that had absolutely no effect upon the girl. She just went on crying.

The train was soon packed with children, many of whom hung out of carriage windows laughing, shouting, and saying their goodbyes while others, mirroring their parents, wept and begged to be allowed to stay.

There came the sound of banging doors followed by a loud blast on a whistle and with a sudden explosion of steam from the engine followed by a strong jolt, the train began to move slowly out of the station. Last hugs were given and received before arms slid from around the necks of loved ones and wet cheek unglued itself from wet cheek, sad face from sad face, leaving only clasping hands to bridge the gap between the old world of familiar and the new world of unknown before they too were forced apart by the movement of the train, and all that remained were the last echoing cries of farewell.

"Bye." "God bless you." "Don't forget to write as soon as you arrive." "Muumm! I don't want to go. MUUMM." "See you soon." "Look after yourself." Calls and pleas echoed around us until they became lost in the steamy rattle and clatter of the carriages as the train gathered speed.

Through the carriage window, above the children waiting for their train to arrive, we could see the faces of mothers and fathers shining beneath the wetness of their tears. We waved to them as we passed and some of them waved back until the forward movement of the train took them from our sight.

Although none of us knew it, with the first slow turning of the engine's wheels came the end to a way of life to which many of us would never return and the beginning of a totally different way of life among people, places, sounds and smells that many of us would embrace with total joy.

Slowly at first then more quickly, the platform began to fall behind us. As we came out from under the station canopy George pointed. "There's the bridge," he said, "Look out for mother."

Pressing my face to the window I looked as hard as I could. All I saw was a sea of faces beneath raised arms and waving hands. I never did see her.

As our train rocked its way over the points that took it from one track to another, other engines waiting to collect carriages of their own called out their goodbyes with loud blasts on their whistles. At last we came out of the jumble of criss-crossing rails and onto the line that would lead us eventually to our destination.

Spreading out on either side of the track London lay like a dull and dirty blanket carelessly thrown down. From factories and houses, chimney smoke wrote its disapproval of the coming war with sooty fingers, while glass in the windows of homes and offices flashed in anger at our leaving as we passed.

Overhead floated an armada of barrage-balloons in a variety of changing silvers and oranges, reds and golds, as the wind, that soon would gale fire-filled destruction across Europe, breathed softly on those silent sentinels to our safety across the blue face of late summer's sky.

*   *   *

TWO

Once we had left the sprawl of London behind, the train chattered its way through the strange land that lay outside the carriage windows. Faces, with noses pressed flat against the glass, stared out at a world that few of us had ever seen and which many never knew existed. A land that, stretching out invisible arms drew me to it and, by so doing, made me forever its prisoner.

Fields and hedges that seemed to go on forever replaced the dirty, much begrimed houses and streets of the city. Cows and horses and sheep took the place of the human livestock we had been used to. Horse-drawn carts rocking gently and quietly along narrow country lanes and tracks, replaced the noisy tram cars rushing along city streets that led to nowhere. Orchards full of fruit laden trees beckoned to us, then waved goodbye as we travelled past without stopping.

Sometimes a bunch of cows would go tearing away across the fields as the train approached, their tails in the air. We were never sure if they were racing us or running away in fear.

We watched the birds move effortlessly from one stand of trees or hedge to another while all the time keeping pace with us, the shadow of the train made its own undulating way across the uneven ground that lay beyond the carriage window.

The slow, rhythmical swaying of the train was continually broken as it slowed down or stopped in obedience to signals. On one occasion we slowed down so suddenly that we were all thrown from our seats in a tumble of confusion from which one girl emerged with a bleeding nose. Once we had regained our seats Mrs Farthing gave the girl a handkerchief to hold to her nose, then gave each of us a sweet from a bag she had in her pocket.

She was the first war casualty we had seen. The second was one of the boys who had his head out of the window when a tiny piece of cinder from the engine landed in his eye which sent him reeling back into the compartment hands against his face, making the weirdest of noises. Eventually, after much drama, Mrs Farthing, by using the corner of his handkerchief, managed to remove the offending object, leaving him to nurse a swollen and greatly reddened eye.

At one place where we stopped we were given lemonade to drink and sandwiches to eat. Gifts received with grateful thanks by those who had eaten all their original sandwiches before we had left the station in London.

As it began to grow dark the blinds were pulled down at all of the windows which, because the light in the ceiling of the compartment was weak, left us all sitting in virtual darkness. It also meant we were no longer able to enjoy the countryside passing by outside.

I overcame that problem by lifting the edge of the blind away from the window and immediately received a good telling off from Mrs Farthing who asked, "If I wanted the train to be bombed and everyone killed?" Consequently, I sat for the rest of the journey in a misery of frustration that was not at all helped by George's looks of frowning disapproval.

Finally we reached our destination and climbed from the train into a worse confusion than the one we had left behind in London. There, at least, we had been able to see what we were doing. All that station offered in the way of light came from several hooded paraffin lamps and one or two small torches.

*　　*　　*

The slowness of the journey and the fact that some of the carriages had no corridor, meant many of the children had wet themselves or worse. It was no wonder then that not only did we arrive very tired but that many also arrived in very badly soiled clothes

Often, as no reception or billeting had been organised, church and village halls and schools were used as temporary accommodation and shelter. Bedding, especially in countryside areas, consisted of hay or straw-filled sacks on which to lie with another empty sack for a cover. Food was mainly milk to drink, bread and cheese, with no butter or margarine to eat, to which was sometimes added an apple.

Children, mothers and teachers, lived under such conditions for up to a week before they were found billets in the very often, unwelcoming homes of the local populace.

Although no billets had been arranged for us, we were not subjected to straw-filled sacks on the floor of some hall or other, though that would have been far better than the house we found ourselves in.

After what seemed hours, during which time every effort was made to get us into some semblance of order, we were led from the dark station out into an even darker night where after a journey of stumbles, bumps and knocks, we came to a wooden hut at the edge of a field. Inside we were told to sit down and be quiet. As there were few chairs, most of us ended up sitting on the floor.

I remember how we felt that night as a procession of people came into the hut and looked us over. It was as though we were not real children at all, but items being selected in order to make life easier for those doing the choosing.

Many accompanied their choice with comments such as 'I'll take the girl. She doesn't look as if she'll eat a lot and she'll be a good help to the wife,' or 'This one looks like a strong lad. He'll earn his keep easy enough.'

More than half the children had been taken away before a tall woman, with a most unfriendly look on her ferret-sharp face, came in, and we had our first sight of Mrs A. She stood for some time pinning us with her stare then she said, "I'll take that one," and pointed at George, who immediately stood up telling me to do the same.

"Not both of you," she said, "just you," pointing again at George.

"I can't go without my brother," George told her. "Mother told me that I was to look after him and not let him out of my sight."

"Don't you dare answer me back," she snapped at him. "I don't care what your mother told you. She's not here now so you'll do as I say. Now pick up your things and come along with me."

George, however, was adamant. He'd promised mother he would keep me with him and that was what he intended to do, and no amount of telling or threatening was going to make him change his mind. After a lengthy and very heated discussion between Mrs A and a man, it was decided that they would allow us to stay together and so, picking up our cases, we followed her from the hut.

We trailed after her through the thick darkness for quite a distance before turning in at a gate and following her up a path and into her house, where she took us into the kitchen. Leaving us standing in the weak jaundiced light of a paraffin lamp, she went out and up the stairs. We heard her moving about for a while then the dull clump of her feet as she came back down again.

Back in the kitchen she told us to put the bags we had been given at the station in London on the table, from which she took the tins of food and put them into a cupboard. She then gave us a cup of something to drink and something that looked like cold mashed potatoes to eat.

Much to her great anger and annoyance we left both the food and cup of whatever it was. Not because we weren't hungry, we were. It was just that neither of us was able to swallow anything.

Lighting a candle she led us, in a very bad mood, out of the kitchen and upstairs into a small bedroom that held the single bed in which we were both to sleep. George asked her where the toilet and bathroom were. She answered by reaching under the bed and drawing out a white enamel chamber pot with a red handle.

"This is what you use. I'll show you where to empty it in the morning." She left us then without saying goodnight and taking the candle with her leaving us to undress and get into bed in the dark.

Despite the long and tiring journey sleep eluded us, and we lay for quite a while talking in hushed tones about the day's events. About mother and our brother Ted, only four months old, and what was going to happen to them and us.

We talked of our house and garden and Mr and Mrs Bunyan who lived next door. We talked about Tom a friend of ours who lived across the street from us with his parents and sister Dawn, who was sixteen and worked in a shop. She had told me that she was going to marry me when I grew up. After that I never went near Tom's house without first making sure that Dawn was nowhere around.

Above all, the thing that was most vivid to me about the day was not the long hours we had waited for our train to arrive; neither was it the people, the noise, nor the to-ing and fro-ing as bodies pushed against bodies in order to get where they had been directed. It wasn't the sad faces, the glad faces, the smiles or the tears. It wasn't the tiredness or the crush, but the smells. Those ageless, timeless, smells of steam and fumes, oil and smoke, wet coal and hot ashes, all wrapped around the smell of passengers and carriage dust. They were the last things I was aware of before sleep finally overtook me.

*   *   *

The harsh, strident, tones, of Mrs A's voice telling us to "Get up and be quick about it," interrupted the warm comfort of sleep. Getting quickly out of bed we used the chamber pot, then finding nothing we could use in which to wash, I don't remember ever washing myself in that house, we made our way downstairs.

In the kitchen, where the light appeared no friendlier than it had the night before, we were told to sit down and eat our breakfast which consisted of two bowls of bread and milk. From then on we were given the unvaried diet of either bread and milk or several slices of bread and dripping. It seemed to us that they were the only kinds of food left in the world and as neither of us could stomach bread and milk it meant we were always hungry.

Once, when she was frying something that smelled really good we asked if we could have some. A long hard stare was followed by, "Certainly not. Children should never be given meat. Not any kind of meat. It's not good for them."

"Mother gives us meat to eat when we're at home," George informed her. "I'm sure that she wouldn't if it wasn't good for us."

"That shows how much your mother knows about bringing up children and what's good for them to eat doesn't it? I don't care what you eat when you're at home, you'll not be getting any meat in this house." And, true to her word, we didn't.

Living in that house brought us only misery, unhappiness and hunger and did nothing to instil in us a liking, trust or respect, for the strangers who then controlled our lives. We appeared unable to do anything right. Mostly our efforts were rewarded with slaps or shouts for being rude.

I lived with Mrs A for just over two weeks, before the day a man came to the house and with no explanations told me he was taking me away. I started to go and tell George that I was leaving but was told I couldn't. When I tried to the man held me back.

That was the signal for me to begin my own war. Fists, feet and teeth were my weapons which with a few well-placed slaps he quickly neutralised, bringing about my surrender. I never did get to say goodbye to George or even tell him that I was going. Almost two years passed before we saw each other again and by that time we were virtual strangers

The house I was taken to stood by itself at the far end of a large garden. Inside it was miserably dark and dull and full of children and adults who, despite the last few days of late summer coming to the windows to share their soon-to-be-gone warmth and brightness, were always miserable.

It seemed that the grown-ups only pleasure came from slapping and screaming at the children. At night, as all the beds had been taken by the grown-ups and babies, many of us slept on the floor which did nothing to ease our aches and bruises.

I remained in that house for some weeks before mother, who had at last managed to prise out of someone the name of the place to which we had been sent, came to visit us. To say she that was upset at the extreme condition she found me in, is to greatly understate the true anger of her feelings.

I was in a filthy state. Unwashed, my hair crawling with lice and my body more than a little bruised. I was wearing a pair of wellington boots and the same clothes I had worn the day I had been evacuated. My suitcase, with the changes of clothing it contained, along with my shoes and overcoat, we never saw again.

She took me back to London with her that day where she set about the task of returning me to a more clean, healthy and acceptable condition.

*　　*　　*

THREE

The **preparations** that were being made in readiness for the invasion everyone believed would soon arrive from across the Channel, had given the city a very different look when I returned. Everywhere bags had been filled with sand and built around the doorways and windows of hospitals, schools, shops and factories to serve as blast barriers. To these changes was added the blackout that made any journey after dark not only difficult but downright dangerous.

For many reasons it was not possible for mother to keep me with her permanently and so, two weeks after she had brought me home, I found myself once more on a train being taken out of the danger zone to the Wiltshire town of Westbury.

That journey, although punctuated with as many stops and starts as the first one, brought with it several long-lasting memories. The way we crowded every window whenever the train slowed down or stopped to see what was going on. The sight of four or five aeroplanes speeding across the sky to the sounds of our loud cheers and waves which followed them long after they had disappeared over the horizon. Streams, that in the cold Autumn sun, sparkled like silver ribbons. But of all the things we saw and heard, it is a man who travelled in our compartment that I remember most.

He was short and stout and had kind of sticky out ears. His hair, thick at the back of his head and around the sides, was thin and wispy on top, through which his scalp shone pinkly. Not only did he tell us stories and teach us songs, he also made coins and cigarettes appear from and disappear into, the most unlikely places. From beneath our gas masks, from behind our ears, out of our pockets and even, or so it seemed, from the air itself, they came and went with a suddenness that held us all breathlessly captive and captivated.

Arriving at last in daylight this time, we climbed from the warm train onto an autumn-chilled platform, and into a far happier and much better organised reception than the previous one had been. In Westbury we were met by a small

14

group of adults who took us from the station and onto waiting buses which delivered us to the senior school. There we were given cakes and buns to eat and a hot drink, while we waited for someone to come and take us home with them.

*   *   *

The lady who collected me was plump, very comforting and had a smile that took away the apprehension I was feeling. We walked for quite a distance past houses that were either a hideous red-brick in colour, or had been painted in a variety of pastel shades, until we reached the New Town crossroads. There we turned up the hill, beside the small school that I was soon to attend, and carried on to the Butts where my new home was situated.

It was in fact, two semi-detached houses converted into one in order to house more children. There were already quite a few living there when I arrived.

The conditions in that home were different in every way to those I had experienced in the previous two places. From the moment I arrived in Westbury I was well-fed, well cared for and, most important of all, given love. What did it matter that I had to share a bed with another boy? What did it matter that the noise and chatter was too loud at meal-times? I was happy. There was always so much to do both inside the house and out, that boredom was an unknown thing.

The happiness and love I was given left no room for the sad loneliness that had remained with me since leaving mother and my brothers. Where I lived now, surrounded by the space and freedom of the countryside, removed any desire or longing I may still have had to 'go back'.

The people living around us were, for the most part, very friendly, although there were times when we gave them reason not to be. On one occasion one of the boys who had climbed the fence into the next garden to retrieve a ball, was given a resounding clout for his bad manners.

"I don't mind you having your ball back," the owner told him, "but you should have asked for permission before you went stamping all over my garden."

That same man, when Christmas came, gave each one of us a present. Mine was a wooden railway engine painted green and red. A toy I loved and played with for many years.

The winter of nineteen thirty-nine was among the coldest that had been recorded. A fact that went completely unnoticed by us and which did nothing to lessen the joyful exhilaration I felt when we were taken out onto the sloping fields where I went tobogganing for the first time in my life.

When the weather was suitable, some of us would walk to the town with the lady and go round the shops buying whatever was needed. That done we set off home again all of us sharing the task of carrying the bags. On other occasions we would go for walks along the quiet country lanes and past cottages whose flower-filled front gardens made me feel homesick and lonely as they brought back to me strong memories of the garden we had once had.

The walk we all enjoyed the most was when we were taken up on the hills. It was a walk of about a mile that began on a fairly good road, which became a muddy, stone-littered track about halfway up.

Once there, while German forces across the Channel were learning to come to terms with landing men and their machines of war from both genuine and makeshift landing craft as they prepared for their invasion of Britain, I began learning how to come to terms with my new environment of space and light, clean air and freedom.

The boundaries of my world until then had always been determined by the distance between the houses on each side of the street in which we lived, and the streets at either end. Now they reached into the far distance until they faded and disappeared into the hazy shimmer of summer's heat.

On one of our walks we met a man who told us that on one of the slopes there was a white horse.

"Where?" we asked, looking around us.

"Ah! you wunt see'n," he told us, "He's gone into hidin' `til the war be over."

"Why?" we wanted to know.

"Well `tis so they Germans can't spot`n when they d`fly their aeroplanes over here," was his reply.

"What will it do for food?" we asked. "If it's gone into hiding, how will the person who feeds it know where to leave the food?"

"I don't reckon that old horse will be too worried about that," was his laughing reply. "He don't eat much at the best of times."

As we regularly saw other horses in the fields, none of us could understand why it was just the white horse that had gone into hiding or what possible difference it would make if the Germans did see it. We decided there wasn't really a white horse at all. It was just another of the stories the grown-ups seemed to be forever kidding us with.

There was no kidding, however, about the beautiful view from the top of those hills. Below us the valley lay neatly divided into three parts by the road that ran from Westbury to the small village of Bratton three miles away, and by the railway line, along which trains travelled almost non-stop in both directions carrying men and the machinery of war where they were most needed.

*   *   *

I moved from that house into the one next door when Mrs Davis took me in

16

to live with her and her family. I remember that I felt quite grown up when I was given my own bed in a far quieter and less crowded house, although it took me quite a while to get used to it.

The months during which I lived with the Davis family were, at that time, the happiest of my childhood. Mrs Davis, 'Mum' I called her, gave me the same love and care I had been given since my arrival in Westbury, no matter what I had or had not done, as did her husband Mr Davis, a gentle man who I grew to know as 'Pop'.

Beryl, the elder of the Davis daughters, spent hours making up and playing games with the children, of which my favourite was hide-and-seek. Then Beryl would help me into an empty rain-water butt that stood at the side of their house, where I could remain hidden but able to see when the seeker was near through the bunghole in the side of the butt.

Another source of pleasure was helping Pop in the garden, where he taught me how to dig the ground, sow seeds, and set the peas, beans and potatoes, in their drills. I also helped him push the mower when the grass required cutting.

His understanding of children in their search for knowledge was apparent in the way he always did his best to answer the endless stream of questions that I was constantly badgering him with.

School began for me soon after I'd gone to live with the Davis family. Mum took me on my first day and saw me into the playground where, while the other children there played their games, I stood by myself and looked about me.

From the outside the grey stone walls of the school gave it a surprisingly gentle appearance, making it look more like a small church from which the stained glass of its windows had been removed and plain glass put in its place. The tiles, all covered in a greenish-brown moss, gave an air of venerability to the building.

At the west end of the roof was a narrow bell tower, open on two sides, from which hung the bell that in the not too distant past had rung to warn pupils that lessons would soon begin but which then hung in silence as it waited for the peace that would, hopefully, soon return.

Some of the children came over and began speaking to me but for all I understood of what they were saying, they might have been talking double-Dutch. Who knows? Perhaps they were.

The need to make some kind of response was removed when a lady, who I later learned was the Headmistress, came out of the building and called for us to line up quietly before she led us inside. There, after being shown where to hang my coat I was taken to a classroom and introduced to the teacher and my new classmates.

The classroom was quite small and had three windows, one in each wall. The fourth wall was made of a half wood half glass partition, in which the door through which to enter and leave the room was situated. The walls were bare stone on which a map of the World hung beside a map of Great Britain and several very uninspiring pictures.

It was the beams supporting the roof that caught most of my attention. On them were recorded, in large painted letters, some of our history's most important dates and people. The Normans, the Houses of Plantagenet and York and various kings and queens. All placed there no doubt to inspire the raising of our eyes to Heaven in order to find the answers to some of life's more pressing and demanding questions.

Those dates were added to during nineteen-forty by the history that was being made then. In June, the evacuation of our soldiers from the beaches at Dunkirk; in July, the Battle of Britain began and continued until November.

August, and London burned again for the first time since the fire that had begun in Pudding Lane as incendiary bombs, loosed from thousands of feet above the city, rained down on the helpless people below. On the night of seventh/eighth of September the real Blitz of London began. From that night on the bombers came without a break until November the First. November the Second was the first night that passed without a raid.

On Friday the thirteenth of September, Buckingham Palace was hit. An incident that prompted one of the local worthies to exclaim to Pop, "It's a good job they bombs didn't hurt their Majesties, or they Germans would have found themselves in real trouble. We wouldn't have sat back and let them away with a thing like that."

Not all of the bombs fell on London. The area around us had its fair share. There were raids on Somerset and Bristol in August and September, with a heavy one on the twenty-fifth of September on Filton which caused great loss of life and an immense amount of damage and destruction.

*   *   *

Despite all that was happening to the people and places close to us, it did not appear to have any affect on, or make any difference to, our lives. Hours ran into days, days into weeks, with only the local language causing me problems, that led some of the children to observe, "Don't he speak funny?" It was a problem, that in the way of children was quickly overcome, so that in no time at all I was `oohin' and `arrin' like a native Wiltshire son, born and bred.

I was involved in several incidents, one of which took place on my way home from school one day at lunchtime. It was the growing season and everything in the garden was coming along nicely including two rows of carrots which, for some unknown reason, absolutely fascinated me.

Whatever it was, that day I went along both rows of carrots carefully pulled them up and lay them neatly on the ground. That done, I carried on up to the house and into the kitchen where Mum and Pop were sitting at the table.

"You'm a bit late today," she greeted me.

"I know," I said. "That's because I've got a really nice surprise for you."

"Oh! What's that then?"

"You'll have to come down the garden to see it," I told her turning to go out again.

"Will it keep `til we've finished eating?" Pop asked.

I reluctantly assured him that it would as long as we didn't take too long.

"Right. You eat your dinner and I'll finish mine, then we'll go and have a look at what `tis you've got down there."

I did as he told me, but I was so excited I don't think I ever ate a meal as quickly in my life.

As soon as we were finished we walked down the garden to where the carrots lay in all their orange coloured glory. I pointed to them proudly.

"There you are," I said, "my surprise. What do you think of it?"

I watched as he stood in silence looking at them. He looked for what seemed to be hours, and the longer he looked the less sure I became of the value of my surprise.

Finally, unable to bear the silence any longer, I asked, "Don't you like it? I thought that a big surprise like that would make you happy."

Crouching down beside me he pulled me to him and put an arm round my shoulders. "Like it?" he said. "Course I like it. And you'm right `tis a big surprise. I've had a few surprises in my life, more than I can count, but I've never had one like this. I just don't know what to say."

19

He sent me to fetch the vegetable basket and together we put the carrots into it. That done, I carried them up home where I proudly presented them to Mum. Nothing more was ever said about my 'surprise'. Perhaps it left them speechless.

Several times Pop took me with him when he went to work. He worked on the railway and had a hut alongside the track where he and his mate sat to have their breaks.

I loved being in that hut and hearing the rails 'singing', signalling the coming of a train long before you could hear the train itself. Then, what began as a soft hum in the far distance would grow louder until with a 'SWOOSH' the train would thunder past, making the hut vibrate so much that the cups would dance a jig across the table, and we would have to hold onto them to prevent them being shaken right off.

Once or twice I was given a special treat when I rode with them on a hand-operated machine they used on line inspection. It was propelled by the two men pumping handles up and down on either side of a central pivot, which operated the driving gear. The speed of the machine depended on the rate at which the two men worked the handles.

When they came to a part of the line requiring attention, they would stop the machine, climb off, and do whatever was needed, such as taking a long-handled spanner with which they tightened the nuts on the 'fishplates' that secured the ends of each length of rail together. On other occasions I would go with them as they walked the track, making sure the wooden blocks holding the rails in place in the metal 'chairs' were secure.

*   *   *

The last day I was to live in Westbury though I was unaware of the big change about to take place in my life, began no differently to any other day. I ate my breakfast, kissed Mum, and set off for school, where the morning passed without mishap.

It was at lunchtime that things began to get completely out of hand, when I ran out of the playground and straight into a man who was cycling down the hill. Luckily neither of us was hurt, although the man was sent flying from his bike and landed in the hedge. While people ran to his assistance, I was hauled back into the school.

There my gross stupidity, lack of thought, and general all-round low level of intelligence, were made known to me in a series of high-pitched shouts and screams. Punctuated and impressed upon my hands through the medium of the cane, they carried with them the message that it was only through pain that I could ever attain the necessary standards that life in general, and the school in particular, required of me.

With those words of adult wisdom ringing in my ears, I was allowed to continue my interrupted journey home for lunch.

When I arrived Mum was in such an excited state that she made no comment on my late arrival. I had not even washed my aching hands when she took me by the shoulders. "You wait 'til you see the surprise that's come for you," she said.

"What is it?" I asked.

"Something very special," she answered. "You go on through the best room and see."

Doing as she said I went through to the front room. A lady, dressed in a dark brown coat and wearing a hat with one of those veils that just covered the eyes, was sitting on one of the chairs beside the table. Apart from that, nothing in the room seemed any different. Certainly nothing that made me think it was special.

Mum Davis came into the room and stood beside me.

"What do you think of your surprise then?" she asked me. "You know who this lady is, don't you?"

I looked at the lady again. I had no idea who she was and said so.

"Course you do," said Mum. "That's your mother."

"Mother?" I echoed. "My mother! She's not my mother. You're my mother."

"But this lady is your real mother. She's come to take you home with her."

I looked at her, stunned into disbelief. What had I done to make her send me away with a stranger? Had knocking that man off his bicycle been bad enough for that? A sudden lump in my throat blocked all the questions I wanted to ask.

Turning, I went out into the kitchen and sat on the back step and began waiting for Pop to come home. I knew that once I told him the story he'd soon put things right. There was no way he would let any strange lady take me away with her, no matter who she said she was.

Mum Davis came and sat down beside me.

"Listen ..." she began, but I interrupted her.

"When's Pop coming?" I asked.

"He's not coming in for his dinner today," she answered. "He's away up the line working.

After a while she said, "Listen, that lady really is your mother you know. That's why she's come to take you home with her. I'm sure you'd like that, wouldn't you?"

"I'm not going anywhere with her," I said, still looking down the garden for Pop. "I'm staying here with you. She can get someone else to take home."

We sat together in silence then Mum said, "Wouldn't you like to go on the train with her? If you did, you could show her your hut."

Of all the things she could have said, that was the one guaranteed to get my immediate attention; it was a suggestion that could not be answered with a quick No! It required very serious thought. I was very proud of that hut and knew that I would enjoy showing it to the lady. There was also the added bonus of going on a train. I was about to agree when another thought struck me.

"What about school?" I asked her, squeezing my sore hands together. "I'll be in trouble if I'm late."

"Don't you go worrying your head about no school," she told me. "I'll see about that and explain things. You wont get into any trouble, I promise."

"Alright then," I agreed, "I'll go on the train with her and show her my hut, but you better tell her that I've got to be back in time for my tea."

"Good boy," said Mum, hugging me. "Now come on up to the table and eat your dinner."

The meal was followed by a bath and change of clothes, a huge hug from Mum that made my face all wet and then, with my real mother, I left the Butts for the last time. Together we walked down the hill past the school and on down to the Market Place. From there a bus took us to the station where several trains came and went before ours pulled in.

The journey turned out to be a very pleasant once my real mother had convinced me that's who she was. We talked about many of the things we had done and places we had been before the war had interrupted our lives.

She was pleased to see my hut and hear about all the things I had been doing, while she pointed out many things that were of interest to a young boy. I told her the things I had been learning at school, leaving out all reference to bicycles and canes.

As the time passed, so too did the strangeness of being with someone who I was having to get to know all over again. By the time we had reached the small Somerset mining town of Radstock, I was completely at ease with her and found I liked her very much. So much so, that any worry I had that I would not be back in Westbury in time for tea, had gone out of my mind completely.

*   *   *

FOUR

Due to the ferocity of the Blitz, when like thousands of other people she had lost her home to the bombs, mother had been forced to leave London. As little or no effort was made to reunite families, although in truth it would have been an almost impossible undertaking, mother found herself with Ted, our younger brother, travelling by train to Somerset.

On the journey down to the West Country she met a woman called Mrs Clancy who had a son the same age as Ted. That meeting was to prove the beginning of a long friendship between them.

They arrived at the Spa station in Bath a dispirited, tired and unhappy assortment of mothers, older children, infants and babies-in-arms, the latter demanding with loud-voiced insistence that they be fed. From the station a group of them including mother and Ted, were taken by bus to the village of Shoscombe some eight miles away, where they were delivered to the Apple Tree public house. Owned at that time by Mr and Mrs Drew, it was one of several places that had been pressed into service as a reception and distribution centre for evacuated families.

The task of getting the mothers and children billeted fell mainly on Mr Riddick the local councillor, Mr Bending the Headmaster of the school, Mr White, the assistant master and Mr Drew, ably assisted by Mrs Drew and Mrs Riddick.

It proved to be a long, tiring process, for all concerned, which was not helped by the reasons given by some of the villagers as they showed their reluctance to having total strangers in their homes. One woman gave as her reason the fact that she and her husband had just bought a new suite for the parlour "And as we baint gwanna use it, it dunt seem right to ask us to let others use it, 'specially as we dunt even know'm."

Another one claimed that "Thik dog of mine'll get upset if I d'have young'uns runnin' wild all over the place, and I baint gwanna have'n upset. Any road, tidn't as though they be family."

Others were much more forthright in their opposition to having strangers in their homes. A fact that mother was made painfully aware of.

Given the name of a family and directions on how to get to their house, she was told to go there and inquire if they would take her. Carrying Ted she set off and arrived at the house, nearly a mile distant from the Apple Tree, very tired and close to tears, and knocked on the door. A curtain at the downstairs window was drawn back a little and a face stared out, studied her for a while, before the curtain was allowed to fall back into place.

She knocked again and after waiting for some time, the door was opened by a woman whose face was anything but happy or welcoming. She stood looking at mother and Ted for a while before she spoke.

"Yes?"

Mother explained that she had just arrived from London and had been given her name and address as a possible billet. A long silence followed, then the woman said, I'll tak' the babby," reaching out to take Ted, "but I baint takin' you. I baint havin' any of you foreigners in my 'ouse."

Having been separated from George and me at the start of the war, there was no way that she was about to be separated from Ted so, thanking the lady, mother began her journey back to the Apple Tree. There the worry and tiredness overcame her and she broke down in tears.

A tall lady who was talking to Mrs Clancy came over, sat down and put her arm round mother's shoulders. Waiting until the tears stopped she asked what was wrong. When mother had explained the lady said, "Mrs Clancy tells me that you know each other, so if you don't mind sharing a room with her and her babby, you'm more than welcome in my home."

That lady was Mrs Weeks, my much loved 'Auntie Weeks', the nicest, kindest, person I ever knew, who with her husband and family lived in a bungalow at Braysdown. It was there mother took me on the day she brought me home from Westbury.

*　　*　　*

It was dark when we arrived at Radstock making the bus ride to Peasedown, because of the rows of large trees on both sides of the road, seem like a journey through a long tunnel. We left the bus at the Red Post Inn and from there we walked through the cold darkness to Braysdown and the bungalow.

As we walked along Braysdown Lane, there came several brief flashes followed by a weak light as Mr Weeks, who had come to meet us, lit the carbide lamp he used underground in the pit to guide us when he heard us coming.

Taking my case from me, he guided us along the track that led to the bungalow. There he took us into the living-room where Auntie Weeks was waiting with

Mrs Clancy and Barbara, the youngest of the Weeks children.

Auntie Weeks was a tall woman, with a smile that wrote welcome all over her face. I liked her the moment I first saw her with a liking that was soon to turn to love.

Mrs Clancy was a nice friendly person with dark brown eyes and dark, almost black, hair. She was about the same age as mother but slimmer in build.

Barbara was a pretty girl and became like a big sister, but without the bossiness that most older sisters seemed to enjoy visiting upon the younger members of the family. Neither did she ever threaten me with marriage.

She played endless games with me, mainly dressed in her nurse's uniform and wrapping me in yards of bandage. She also taught me how to ride a bike.

There were four Weeks children. Ray and Les the sons and another daughter named Betty. Children is a misleading way to describe them, for at that time both of the sons were in the Royal Navy; Ray in the Mediterranean, while Les was in the colder waters of the North Atlantic and Arctic, escorting the convoys. Betty was away from home in domestic service.

Sitting down at the table, Auntie served us both big helpings of the rabbit stew she had cooked for us. While we ate, I related what Mrs A had said about meat being bad for young children.

"Course 'tidn't bad for them," I was told. "That's how they d'grow up big and strong. Plenty of meat and plenty of milk, with plenty of sleep and crusts. You got to eat your crusts mind, else your bones'll go like rubber and you'll wobble all over the place when you d'walk."

The stew was followed by home-made jam on toast, that was made by putting a slice of bread on a long-handled fork, then holding it in front of the fire until the required level of brownness was reached. That was the first time I had ever seen toast made in that manner, and what made it even better was being allowed to sit in front of the fire and make my own, toasting my face at the same time.

*   *   *

I don't remember going to bed that night but I do remember, quite clearly, waking up the next morning alone in a strange room, full of strange noises coming in through the open window. As I could hear no voices, I thought that everyone had gone off and I had been forgotten.

Not bothering to dress, I went in search of company. To my great relief I found mother and Auntie Weeks sitting with Mrs Clancy at the table in the living-room. They laughed when I related my fears to them, but a hug from mother assured me that she would not be going off and leaving me again.

After I had eaten my breakfast I went with Auntie Weeks out into the garden where the cause of the strange noises I had heard from the bedroom was made known to me...HENS. At first I thought there were hundreds of them, when in fact there was only about thirty at the very most.

In those days hens or bantams were kept by most of the people living in the countryside. Many also kept some ducks, geese or turkeys. Some where the size of their land permitted kept some of each, along with goats, pigs and calves. Auntie Weeks kept only hens.

At first I was terrified of those squawking, clucking birds who seemed to be forever fluffing their feathers and flapping their wings. They all seemed to take great delight charging at me every time I entered their run to feed them. Attitudes that only served to make me run away from them as fast as I could; an action that availed me nothing, for no matter where I ran they followed me. The more daring of them would flap themselves up onto the rim of the bucket and begin feeding there, making me drop it and leave them to it, while Auntie stood laughing telling me to stand still. Fat chance there was of that happening.

Once I realised that they presented no danger, I began to look forward to the ritual of feeding them and collecting the eggs. Sometimes, an ill-tempered one would peck my hand as I pushed it under her to take the eggs from the box, but I soon became used to that and paid it no heed.

Different times of the year brought with them different kinds of feeding for the hens. In the warm weather, when the hens were in lay, they would be fed mainly on corn. In colder weather they would be given boiled potato peelings mixed with a coarse brown powder called mash.

In addition to their regular feeding, they also received a regular supply of grit to help them to produce strong-shelled eggs. The grit was obtained each day from the fireplaces in the bungalow where every morning, before lighting the fires, the ashes from the previous day would be lifted into a bucket kept for that purpose and carried outside. On the way out we would take the sifter, a circular band of wood four inches wide and about two feet in diameter, with a small mesh wire bottom, from its nail in the scullery.

In the hens' run some ashes would be tipped into the sifter which would then be shaken, allowing the dust and small bits of ash to fall through the mesh, to be

picked by the hens. The pieces called 'rubble' that were too large to pass through the mesh, were taken back indoors and used again on the fires.

When one of the hens showed signs of going 'broody', the box kept for the purpose would be made ready. First it had to be washed with warm soapy water and disinfectant, that was my job, then left to dry. Once dry fresh straw would be put in, on top of which Auntie placed the eggs she had selected.

The broody hen would then be removed from the main run and, with much angry clucking, wing flapping and pecking, put into the brood box. There, for the next twenty-one days, she would remain incubating the eggs, arranging them and turning them as and when it was needed. Food and water were put just out-side the box, but close enough that the hen could reach them.

I could hardly contain my excitement when hatching day drew near, and was continually going out to check if anything had happened. At last the chicks would appear, wriggling free of the shell in newborn wetness that dried to give them the appearance of yellow fluff-balls, from which came a non-stop cheeping as they ran to keep up with their mother.

If we were lucky all twelve of the eggs would hatch, but that was a rare occurrence; mostly nine or ten was considered a successful brood. Sometimes, for no apparent reason, the hen would go 'off' the brood part way through the sitting that resulted in the entire clutch of eggs being lost.

A thing I found strange about most of the hatchings I was involved with was the fact that there always seemed to be one chick that required extra attention. That one would be taken into the house and put in a cardboard box beside the fire and fed on bread and milk.

Many times, despite all of the careful attention, the chick died. If it survived it was kept indoors until it was strong enough to be put out into the small rearing run with the rest of the chicks from the same brood. There they remained until they were big enough to be introduced to the main run.

After a week or ten days, the chicks would begin to show their feathers, those at the wing-tips and at the end of the tail appearing first, quickly followed by the body feathers until, in no time at all, they had changed from bright yellow chicks into brown or white or speckled birds.

The hens were not confined to the run all of the time. On many occasions the door of the run would be left open and the hens allowed to range freely in the area at the back of the bungalow. Sometimes one of them would go off by herself and lay her eggs in a secret place instead of in the laying box in the hen house. That provided another source of adventure as I helped Auntie to track down the hidden eggs as though we were hunting for pirate gold.

*   *   *

FIVE

The bungalow stood at the foot of a batch, known as the Big Batch, at one end of a long meadow. Batch is the name given in the Somerset mining areas to the huge, ugly mounds of rock and other waste material brought up from underground and deposited on the surface.

Most of the batches in the area had been planted with fir trees for several good reasons. They were quick growing, which made them an excellent source of ready timber needed to support the roof underground and their tall, straight trunks, made them ideal for use as telegraph poles which provided the owner with another source of income. That they also brought the benefit of giving colour and cover to the ugliness of those man-made mountains would, in all probability, not have been high on the mine-owners list of major priorities when they had been planted.

The Big Batch gave us an exciting and ready-made place on which to learn, practise and perfect, the games and skills that many other children would never know or enjoy. The art of tree-climbing later gave way to more daring pursuits as we grew older. That batch, up the sides of which we learned how to hill-climb, later became the training ground for what was planned to be the very first successful ascent of Everest.

It was also a place where we could go tobogganing every day of the year using anything that was suitable, such as an old tin tray, a smooth-bottomed bath, or a piece of discarded conveyor belt brought up from underground. As long as it was guaranteed to take us from the top of the batch to the bottom and do so in the shortest time possible, we used it.

Carrying our 'toboggans', we would clamber to the top of the batch where, sitting in or on our chosen vehicle, we would come sliding down at great speed. Our only method of steering the course that weaved in and out of the trees was the way we moved our bodies.

These right and left movements had to be timed, for any mistimed swerves carried the possibility of a sudden introduction to one or more of the trees. Several times such meetings had been rewarded with a painful trip to the doctor. It was only our extreme good fortune that none of us finished up in the cemetery.

Those machines, by their very nature, did not have many of the refinements or fittings that were to be found on similar vehicles. To be truthful they had none. Each descent depended on skill and the four-lettered word HOPE. If luck was on our side, we made it safely to the bottom without being stopped by the trees or, the most embarrassing thing of all, falling off. Was the Cresta Run ever more exciting?

A game I was 'conscripted' into, and played with little in the way of enthusiasm was 'wounded soldiers'. Barbara, who had nurses uniform, would wrap me up in bandages and push me around the outside of the bungalow in a large dolls pram with my legs dangling over the sides.

At the back of the bungalow she would lift me out of the ambulance, as she called it, and deposit me on a hospital bed that looked, and felt, like a pile of straw on the ground. Conditions were certainly hard for wounded soldiers in those days.

One day her pram pushing reached new heights when, to my great embarrassment, she pushed me around the batch as far as the gug to meet Uncle Gilb coming off shift from the pit. The things some of the miners said to me made me squirm. I don't remember Uncle Gilb saying anything comforting either.

The gug was a narrow-gauge tramway down which the tubs of coal were sent by means of a steel rope from the pithead at Braysdown to the main L.M.S. railway line at Writhlington in the valley bottom. Reaching the screens the coal was tipped into the waiting main-line trucks, which then carried it to depots throughout the country.

To get from the bungalow to Braysdown Lane the gug had to be crossed. Not difficult when the gug was idle and the rope was still but virtually impossible when it was in use, for due to the steepness of the slope down into the valley the rope would sometimes leap eight or ten feet into the air before it came smashing back against the ground. It took very little imagination to visualise what could happen should anyone be attempting to cross at the wrong time.

I had been warned that not only was I never to cross the gug on my own, but that I was never to go anywhere near it. Warnings which were completely forgotten the day I went by myself to meet Uncle Gilb.

I think I must have been mesmerised by the twin sets of rails that shone like silver snail trails before disappearing over the crest of the hill, for not only did I go to the gug, I also crossed over from the bungalow side and walked beside the rails up towards the pit. Halfway there I met a group of miners, Uncle Gilb among them, on their way home.

I stopped and stood looking at him, a grin of welcome on my face. The look on his face dimmed somewhat the brightness of my smile. The tone of his voice when he spoke, removed it altogether.

"Wass thou doin' here then?" he asked.

"I came to meet you," I answered.

"And how did you get over on this side of they rails?"

I was about to tell him when all the warnings I had been given came flooding back. It was also then that the sky fell on me. For days afterwards I felt it would have been a lot less painful if I had been hit by the gug rope.

*   *   *

The calm, unhurried life we lived was interrupted when Ted, our young brother, was rushed to the hospital at Paulton with suspected spinal meningitis. Days and nights of extreme worry had to be endured by mother and Auntie Weeks, as they waited for the doctor's diagnosis. A worry that had not been eased by the nurse who came in the ambulance and whose only words to mother as she took Ted from her arms was that he would, in all probability, be dead before they reached the hospital. Thankfully, that proved not to be the case.

At the hospital mother was told it would be several days before the results of tests they had to carry out were known, and that they would inform her immediately if any change took place in his condition, Until then, she was not to return to the hospital.

Long nights followed long days of waiting, relieved only by the telephone calls, one a day, that mother was allowed to make. Finally, after two weeks, she was told that she would be allowed in to see him, but for a few minutes only. From then on, three times a week, mother either walked or went by bicycle from the bungalow to the hospital, a distance of some six miles in both directions.

Despite the upset Ted's illness brought, life went on as did the war. On the night of the fourteenth/fifteenth of November, Coventry was bombed in one of the worst raids on a city throughout the entire war.

November the twenty-fourth saw the war brought closer to us as parachute flares lit up Bristol to help the bombers to drop their loads with greater accuracy. They returned again on the second of December to add to the destruction. To the difficulties the firemen faced from burning buildings was the added problem, due to the winter of nineteen-forty being so cold, of the water freezing in the pipes and fire hoses.

Christmas Day. The war was pushed into the background by the rustle of wrapping paper being taken off presents. Along with the box of paints from Auntie Weeks and the cap gun from Uncle Gilb, I also received a clockwork car that had been made in Germany.

Dinner-time was preceded by the smells of roast chicken, sage and onion stuffing and Christmas Pudding, drifting from room to room like invisible, but very welcome, friends. The moment when we would sit at the table and begin eating seemed to take forever to arrive.

Teatime saw the Christmas cake given pride of place on the table, around which plates of sandwiches and mince pies stood guard, while jellies shivered gently in their red and yellow finery beside crackers waiting to be pulled.

Afterwards, sitting round the fire, the grown-ups told us stories of Christmases they had known and the things they had done when they were the age we were then. Of course, the ones we liked the best were the ghost stories. Going to bed later was accompanied by a great deal of nervous laughter and looking over the shoulder, as the candle brought the ghosts we had heard about into the room where, in the flickering light, they danced across the floor and onto the wall beside our beds

*   *   *.

1941. Friday, January the Third. The New Year was less than three days old when Bristol wrote into the record book the most unwanted episode in its history. For twelve hours, beginning at 6.20p.m. until 6.30a.m. on Saturday, when the 'All Clear' siren sent its mournful voice out over the death and debris filled streets of the city, the people had endured what was the longest aerial attack in history.

During the bombing, among a group of people in one of the shelters were two girls, one aged about eleven, the other a little younger. As the attacks grew heavier, the younger of the girls began to cry.

"What's up with you then?" asked the older girl.

"We're all going to be killed," sobbed the younger one. "Those bombs are going to kill us all."

"I reckon you must know Hitler then," said the older girl.

The girl stopped crying for a moment.

"No I don't," she said.

"Well does he know you?"

"Course he doesn't."

"Then you can stop crying. You'm safe enough."

"How does that make me safe?" the young one wanted to know.

"Because," the older girl told her, "My dad said that if a bomb has got your name on it, it'll get you. But seeing as how Hitler doesn't know yours he's not going to be able to put it on one of his bombs, is he? And if there isn't a bomb with your name on it you'm safe. So like I said, you can stop all that crying and carrying on."

The sixteenth of January. An escaping bomber jettisoned its load of death over Bath causing the first fatalities of the war in the city. One family, sent out of London for their safety, was killed outright. In the street outside the house, two men were killed by flying debris. Several months later, on Good Friday, the same thing happened, resulting in eleven deaths.

*   *   *

As the weather improved and got less cold, I began going with Auntie Weeks and mother on Saturday mornings to the market at Radstock that was held in a large building standing at the town end of Waterloo Road opposite the L.M.S. Station.

Inside that building it was as though Aladdin's cave had been brought to life. Up each side and down the centre stood stalls that appeared to sell everything. Whatever you wanted it seemed possible to obtain inside that 'treasure' house. It was there that the first bicycle I ever owned was bought. Red in colour, it had a bell that rang and a red disc on the back mudguard that glowed warmly in the darkness when light fell on it. I couldn't wait to get it home where, with a good deal of help and patience from Barbara, I learned to ride it.

*   *   *

The days of freedom governed only by the need for food and sleep had, eventually, to come to an end, when the time for me to return to school arrived. It was a time I felt sure was bringing to an end forever, the happy days I had known since my arrival at the bungalow.

"Don't talk so soft," said Auntie, when I told her how sad I was feeling. "You've got to go to school. Everyone's got to go to school."

"Why?" I wanted to know.

"So's they can learn all the things they got to know about, that's why," she told me.

"But why can't I stay here and you 'learn' me?" I asked.

"Because I don't have the time, that's why. 'sides, I'm not one of they teachers. You got to be clever and know a lot to be one of they. You go to school and listen to everything that you'm told, and you might learn enough to be a teacher yourself when you d'grow up. That'd be a sight better than going to work down a pit."

I left her and went out to Uncle Gilb who was working in the garden. Seeing the misery on my face, he stopped what he was doing.

"Wass up wi' you then?" he asked. "You d'look as if you got a nail sticking up in your boot that's givin' thee jip."

"No I haven't," I said.

"Well somethin's not pleasin' thee," he said. "You've got a face on thee like a cracked dinner plate."

"It's because I've got to go back to school again," I told him.

"And that's why you'm wearin' that daft look? I wish I were goin' back to school instead of down that pit, I'll tell thee that. You wouldn't hear I complainin'. You d'want to start feelin' happy about it not acting as if the world were gwanna end any moment."

"But why do we have to go to school?" I asked him.

"Because that's the law and 'tis no use moanin' and goin' on about it. 'sides, if you dunt go to school you'll always be as daft as you be now."

That brought to an end our conversation as he went back to the work he'd been doing before I'd interrupted him, leaving me alone with my unhappiness.

*   *   *

SIX

There were many who held the belief that the weather did much to influence the way in which we acted, and reacted, to other people and situations.

"Tis the weather what's at the bottom of it," was the often heard reason for whatever was being commented on. Crops not up to standard or better that had been expected. Too hot, too cold; too wet, too dry; Faces miserable, faces happy. All down to the weather.

Sunny weather was supposed to bring cheerful and happy dispositions. Changeable weather to give rise to changeable and disagreeable dispositions.

That, however, was not always the case, for foul weather often appeared to have no adverse effects on some people and seemed unable to dampen their happy attitudes. Sunny weather on the other hand could, and often did, bring the most curt and miserable of outlooks, such as mine on the day I started back to school.

It was one of those lovely early Spring mornings with the sun, already promising a nice day, bringing happy smiles to the faces around me but having no such effect on mine. I was totally miserable and the sight of Barbara looking as happy as everyone else, added to my dejection. I had expected some sympathy from her; she was after all, having to go to school as well.

My misery was greatly increased by what I considered to be an unnecessary and prolonged assault upon me with soap and water, despite the fact that I had undergone a similar attack in the bath the night before. Soap in the hands of a grown-up must surely be a boy's deadliest enemy.

Finally, despite stretching the elastic of time wasting to the limit during breakfast and later when feeding the hens and collecting the eggs, the time arrived when we had to leave. After suffering the indignity and embarrassment of being kissed and hugged by everyone, I set off with Barbara on my journey back to school.

*   *   *

That morning I crossed the gug for only the second time since my arrival at the bungalow. We continued on round the foot of the small batch until we reached

Braysdown Lane where we turned left and walked towards two rows of cottages that stood about a hundred yards away.

Over the rooftops, the winding gear at the pit could be seen, its two wheels blurring round in opposite directions as coal was brought to the surface in one cage, while at the same time empty tubs were lowered into the pit in the other.

As we walked towards the cottages I noticed that two of them had the castle shapes we drew on our pictures, along the top of the walls where the roofs began. I thought they were real castles and asked Barbara if they belonged to the king. She laughingly assured me that they didn't and that as far as she knew the king still lived in London.

We turned in at the gate of the first castellated house and walked up the path. As we reached the door it was opened by a girl the same age as Barbara whose name was Margaret and who was the eldest of the Weston children. We followed her into the house and into the parlour, where I met her mother and the rest of the family.

Mrs Weston was a tall slim woman, with a gentle smile and a quiet voice. I was to learn later that she also possessed a strong right arm and a long umbrella, with which she seemed able to reach our backsides no matter how much distance we put between ourselves and it. From that first meeting I liked her and was treated by her as one of the family.

She had three sons. John (Jack) was the eldest and who even then was not only a gentleman, but also a gentle man. He is, without doubt, one of the nicest people I have ever known. Next was Bernard, another nice person, who was to become the most popular boy in the school; a fact that was clearly shown the day he was overwhelmingly voted school captain. The third son Frank, was the same age as myself and who, despite all his strenuous efforts to avoid it, was to become my best friend. The baby of the family was Brenda, who was two years old.

My thought that the king owned their house gave them a great deal of amusement. Many times afterwards when I went to call for Frank I would be told, if he was out, that the king was not at home. It became one of those things that seem to become a habit, and from that first day I always referred to the house as Frank's 'castle'.

As soon as the boys had brushed their hair and put on their jackets, we left the 'castle'. Outside we were joined by a girl called Sylvia, who lived in the next rank. Farther back down the Lane, beside the track we had walked along from the bungalow, waited another girl named Vera, with her younger brother Gordon

That walk, filled as it was with the pleasure and peace of the countryside coming back to life after the long winter, was the first of many that made going back to school such a welcome beginning to each day.

*   *   *

As we reached the end of the Lane where, even at that early hour, some of the men, mainly miners, were already hard at work 'digging for victory', a skylark rose up from one of the fields and began singing its way toward the morning sky. Up it climbed on flickering wings growing smaller and smaller the higher it went until it disappeared from our sight and all that was left were the notes of its song, falling gently onto the countryside below like invisible snowflakes resting warmly on our ears.

They too faded until we had to strain to hear them at all then, just as we thought they would fade completely, they began to grow in volume again as the lark began its descent. It became visible again as it came spiralling down until some eight or ten feet from the ground, the sound of its beautiful song stopped and like a bird of prey diving on its quarry, it folded its wings and dropped like a stone.

The sudden dropping we later learned, was one of several defence actions the skylark employed to confuse any watching predator, for it reduced the risk of the nest being found and disturbed or, worse still, being found and any baby birds that might be in it being destroyed.

The Lane ended at the road leading from Writhlington to Peasedown. On the grass verge between the hedge of the allotments and the road, stood half a dozen 'tank traps'. They were large, cylindrical-shaped lumps of concrete, about six feet in length and four feet in diameter which, in the event of an invasion, were to be rolled into the road to halt the progress of the enemy tanks.

However, there was, as there often is with such plans, a problem, for not only did they weigh several tons each, they had also sunk several inches into the ground which would have made it virtually impossible to move them at all, far less to have got them out into the middle of the road. Even if it had been possible, the tanks would simply have bypassed them by driving through the allotments or the field on the other side of the road.

No-one ever questioned the idea behind the traps, for they did make us feel safe and confident that even if enemy tanks reached as far as Braysdown, those traps would ensure they got no farther. Perhaps by so doing, they fulfilled their purpose.

*   *   *

From the top of Rag Hill, the village of Shoscombe could be seen lying in quiet peace along the side of the valley. As far back in history as the Stone Age, people had lived where the village now stood.

How many times had some Neolithic man stood where we stood then, looking down the length of the valley? Although not seeing what we saw, he would surely have looked at the same surrounding landscape whose contours had probably changed very little over the millenniums.

At the foot of the hill, like a sentinel guarding that entrance to the village, stood Wells' farmhouse. At the far end of the village, halfway up White Hill, Mr Bending's house stood aloof and watchful, gazing down on the cottages and people below. Between those village outposts lay the houses among which, depending on your religious persuasion, stood what many considered to be the two most important buildings in the village; the Methodist Chapel and the Apple Tree pub.

The first stood in sombre greyness just below Wells' farm, its large windows frowning darkly upon any sign or form of sinfulness. It seemed to cheer up a little on Sundays when the sound of well-known hymns and psalms were heard echoing out across the village.

The second nestled in the centre of the village where it lay, hidden from the disapproving glare of the chapel by some of the cottages, in the folds of the surrounding fields. The music from that establishment although different, lifted the spirits of those who sang, for the songs brought the same joy and pleasure as singing hymns did to the chapel people.

We walked on down through the village until we came to the cinder path at the foot of White Hill. Hens pecking about in the grass ran from us as though they had never seen children before. Among them were some strange looking birds that were almost round in shape, with bright red faces and wattles and heavily speckled grey and white feathers.

"What kind of hens are they?" we wanted to know.

"They'm not hens," we were told. "They'm Guinea Fowl. Round here we d'call 'em gleanies."

At the far side of the field at the bottom of the hedge that separated it from the next was a two-railed wooden fence and a wicket gate. On the other side of that fence and gate was, in season, the most nut-laden hazel bush in the area.

In the field on the other side of the hedge, a grey pony and a large chestnut coloured cart horse were grazing. As we went through the gate, both animals came walking down to the fence and put their heads over it which, as far as some of us were concerned, effectively barred our way. As they did we saw that the cart horse was blind in one eye.

Seeing our nervousness Frank's sister Margaret, taking my hand said, "Come on over and pat her. She's not going to hurt thee."

She was absolutely right, it wasn't. I wasn't going to get close enough to it. Neither were any of the others.

While she stepped up to the animal and began patting it to show us how gentle it was, we hung back, sure that if we went anywhere near it something dreadful would happen to us. We were even more convinced when it suddenly blew loudly through its nostrils, causing us to jump back in alarm and Margaret and the other girls to burst out laughing.

That was alright by us. If any of them wanted to touch it they could. We only knew that we were not going to.

Although the large horse seemed friendly enough, the pony was altogether different. Bad-tempered and unfriendly it kept stretching its neck out over the top of the fence, making clear its intention of biting anyone who was careless enough to get close to its teeth. It even took several nips at the large horse's neck.

While all the horse patting and stroking had been going on, other children on their way to school had joined us so that there was quite a large crowd of us when we resumed our journey. The path continued on past a small spinney at the top of a field whose sloping side fell steeply to the valley floor below until, immediately behind the Rectory, it turned sharply left to give way in a few yards to the hill that led gently down to the school.

*   *   *

SEVEN

Reaching the foot of the hill I saw for the first time St. Julian's Church of England Elementary School that was to become our Alma Mater and seat of our learning throughout the most formative and impressionable years of our lives. Firstly under the tutelage of Mr Bending, did other children anywhere have a Headmaster such as he? and later under Mr White, who was appointed to the post when Mr Bending retired, but who at that time was the assistant master at the school.

The building was constructed from the lovely grey stone so common to that part of Somerset, and could justifiably lay claim to the title of 'unique', for it was possibly the only building in England that was a school during the week and a church on Sunday. It was in every sense a church school.

The path that led from the road into the playground at the front of the school ran between two hedges. On the right the hedge enclosed a grassy area where the teachers on warm sunny days, would sit during playtime and at lunchtime. To the left was a shrubbery bordered on three sides by a hedge and on the fourth by the school wall. Outside the wall, but close to it, grew a huge horse-chestnut (conker) tree.

The playground when we arrived was filled with children greeting friends and sharing with them all of the experiences and excitement they had encountered and survived, since they had last met. Being part of the new intake of children with no friends to greet, Frank and I stood with our backs resting against the wall of the school a part of, but not yet one of, the blizzard of children that whirled around us.

It was a situation that did not last long for seeing us standing there by ourselves, several of the boys drifted over and began their quest for knowledge and by so doing, broke for us the ice of being 'new' boys.

"Wass thy name then? Where's come from? Hast thou got any brothers or sisters?" Endless questions each seeking an answer, and each answer drawing further into the group until, in no time, we were storming around the playground with them, shouting and calling as loudly as the next.

A man came out of the school and blew a loud blast on a whistle that brought all movement and talk to an end as the children stood quietly waiting. The instruction to "Get into your lines", returned life to motionless limbs as they moved to stand in their respective places. Those of us attending for the first time, stood waiting to be told what to do.

With the words "Lead off" the children began following each other into the building. Once they were inside, the man, Mr White, called the new arrivals to him and together we went with him into the school where the smells of disinfectant and floor polish, so loved by generations of cleaning ladies, filled our nostrils with their never-to-be-forgotten bouquet.

We found ourselves in a big room that, although it was used as a classroom during the week, was in fact the nave of the church. The chancel and altar, closed off from the nave during the week by lowering a wooden roller blind (slats), gave the building the feeling of having been transported from the time when monks were the only teachers and cloisters the only classrooms.

*   *   *

The bare stone walls were relieved by a variety of pictures and framed certificates that told of the school's strong musical background, and the successes of the choirs down the years at the National Eisteddfod. The senior choir had also broadcast on the wireless, the first time being in nineteen thirty-six. The junior choir were to make their debut on the wireless in nineteen forty-one, but due to the war it had to be cancelled.

Hanging on chains from the ceiling that allowed them to be lowered for lighting, paraffin lamps added their oily smell to the warmth of the classrooms, provided by either a stove or a fire. In the case of the big room there was one of each.

When we were all safely inside, we were collected by our new teacher, Miss Chambers, and taken to our classroom. I was happy that Frank and I were to be in the same class.

The teaching staff at that time consisted of Mr Bending, a tall, well-built man, who, due to a wound he sustained during the First World War, walked with a heavy limp. Of all his undoubted abilities as a teacher, it was the magical quality he brought to the reading of stories that made the deepest impression on us. He had the rare gift of making the reading of works such as Three Men in a Boat and Treasure Island, not so much stories we had listened to, but adventures we had all lived through and enjoyed.

Singing periods was another area in which he excelled. The rise and fall of our voices in response to his "Remember the hills and the valleys, the hills and the valleys," were lessons that he always managed to make enjoyable. Then, when the serious singing was over, he always allowed us to let rip with either 'Ten Green Bottles' or 'The Camptown Races'.

In addition to Mr Bending, there was Mrs Bending, Mr White, the assistant master, Miss Chambers and Miss Ferguson, who was also new to the school. She had travelled with a group of evacuees from London and had remained to teach them in order that their education should not be disrupted more than was absolutely necessary.

In the classroom we were told to sit at one of the desks that had been built to accommodate two pupils. Each of the desks had a lift-up top, beneath which was the storage space where we kept books, pencils, pens, rubbers, rulers, comics, and our marbles and conkers. At the top of each desk two ceramic inkwells, kept filled by older children called class monitors, waited in blue-stained whiteness for busy pens.

The first part of that morning was occupied by a series of questions. Name? Address? Age? Had we any brothers or sisters at the school?

Once that was finished we were taken into the cloakroom and each given a peg on which to hang our coats, then outside to the playground and shown how to line up before coming into school. After practising it several times to her satisfaction Miss Chambers took us back to the classroom.

Playtime arrived, and while the calls and chants of games, that sounded like the incantations of witches' covens, flowed over and around the playground like the water of a stream over the pebbles on its bed, Frank and I set off to take a closer look at the school and its environs.

The big playground at the front of the school led onto a large patch of hard-packed earth, made so by the feet of many generations of boys playing football. To the right, alongside the school wall, stood a row of big yew trees beneath which, whatever the weather, the ground was always dry.

It was there when the weather halted all other outdoor pursuits that we played conkers, ball-in-the-hat, toss-ha'penny and marbles, or sat with our Dandys, Beanos, Hotspurs, Rovers and Wizards.

It was the Radio Fun that Eddie Hurden, another of my best friends who, because he rode a Hercules bicycle had been given the nickname of Herksy, and I enjoyed the most. Our favourite was Izzy Bonn and the Finklefeffer family for which nothing ever went right. If it looked, as it sometimes did, that life was about to treat them kindly, they themselves saw that it was doomed to failure.

One of the stories dealt with them having their photographs taken and after the usual series of mishaps they were finally arranged to the photographer's liking. Unfortunately, they had been posed on the trap-door that led to the cellar and as the photographer operated his camera, the trap-door opened and the Finklefeffer family disappeared through it.

The look on Eddie's face as we sat there howling with laughter was so like Jakey Finklefeffer's, that from then on that was what I called him.

Opposite the yew trees on, the other side of the road, was Filer's combined shop and Post Office. There we could buy for a penny, six ice-cream wafers or lemonade crystals in a paper cone, that we dipped up with our fingers and which left both them and our tongues, a deep brownish-yellow for ages afterwards.

Between the patch and the wall running along the back of the school was a sloping area of grass where we played games of stool-ball and rounders or sat, on the warm summer days at lunchtime, and listened to John Arlott's ball-by-ball cricket commentary on the wireless set that Mr Bending brought to school. Beside that grassy area, enclosed behind a wire fence, were the school gardens.

The grassy area was also used when the weather was fine for lessons such as Nature Study and Art, which we did sitting on the grass with our books balanced on our knees. Nature Study often found us walking around the yew trees and hedges, which wasn't nearly as exciting as searching through the grass for the different kinds of insects that lived there.

When we found a really large specimen, especially if it had a lot of legs or did a lot of squirmy wriggling, we would offer it to one of the girls as a token of our affection for them, which usually resulted in them screaming and running away while we chased them to show it would do them no harm.

We knew of course that it was all just an act and that they weren't frightened at all. They just wanted to keep their fondness for us a secret from the rest of the class. Funny creatures girls. We never could understand them.

Often the lesson would be interrupted as planes passed overhead, the roar of their engines drowning out the sound of the teacher's voice. Sometimes, when they flew high up, they looked no bigger than silver full-stops and made no sound at all, leaving only white vapour trails behind them to show the direction they had taken.

At the back of the school another large conker tree, the cause of many weak bladders to pupils of Mrs Bending's class when the conkers were falling, stood in stately splendour. Through the open window, the special sound they made as they hit the ground would send hands shooting up into the air with the plea from their owners that they be excused. Sometimes we would be successful; most times our requests fell on deaf ears.

The worst thing of all, and what made our spirits really sink, was to be late getting out of class for some reason for that meant by the time we got to the tree all the conkers would be resting in the pockets of those lucky enough to get out on time.

It was not long before we met each day with the air of veterans; as though we had always been at the school. Rules, regulations, requirements and the expected standard of effort and behaviour were soon learned. After the first few days the newness of the situation was never a problem and school became, next to our homes, the centre of our lives.

There was no conscious separation of the two for school, like our homes, was never left standing lonely and alone. At the end of each school day and at weekends, it was with us.

At holiday time, especially the long summer holiday, all our high spirits at the prospect of the weeks of freedom that stretched before us were tinged underneath with the sadness that any long parting from a much loved friend always brings. Then, the holiday over, it gave the impression of rejoicing with us as we returned to fill again its welcoming classrooms and playgrounds.

From the beginning I enjoyed every minute of the years I spent at St. Julian's school, as did most of the children who were privileged to attend there. In an age when the cane was synonymous with good manners, intelligence and the ability to learn, it was never used as a threat against us.

Certainly it was used and to very good effect whenever the situation called for it, as quite a few of us were made painfully aware through a series of hand-warming meetings we had with it. Painful though it was, it was still better than the extra homework or punishment lines that were handed out.

It was possible to acquire five hundred of those lines, as I found out on many occasions, with no effort at all. Many of the evenings and weekends of my childhood were spent writing out lines, that all had to done in our best handwriting with correct spelling and punctuation.

*   *   *

There is so much to remember of those happiness-filled years, that it is difficult to know where to begin. The good teaching we received, the kindness of the teachers and their friendship that lasted over the years until sadly, one by one they were no longer with us.

The way the older children, far from pushing the younger ones away, encouraged us to join in their games, which they then modified so that we could enjoy taking part. The feeling of belonging was very strong, for no-one was excluded unless they themselves chose to be.

Most of the games we played were, by their nature, team games. Two things governed when these games were played; the time of the year and the weather. That meant our games were divided into two groups; those we played outside in the playground, and those we played inside in the classrooms.

Football was the most popular outdoor game for the boys, the teams generally being chosen on a fairly flexible basis, although there were times when the 'He's my friend so he's in my team' choice was made.

Probably the most successful way of picking sides came from Gordon (Codger) Young, when the Ferguson tractor came on the market in competition with the Ford. He suggested the sides should be picked on a Ferguson versus the Ford basis and from then on that was the method we used.

Strangely, the two sides usually worked out fairly evenly on a numbers count. Not always of course, for sometimes one or more of the boys would switch their allegiance. Whenever that happened other boys would change sides to even up the numbers and the game would begin.

Next to football the most popular game was one called Bung-the-Barrel. This game needed two sides which had to be not only evenly matched in numbers, but in strength and size as well.

When the choice of which team would be the first to jump had been made, one of the boys from the opposite team would be chosen to be the 'post' and would stand with his back against one of the wooden posts supporting the fence that ran around the school garden. The front boy of the bridge would then put his head into the midriff of the 'post' and hold him tightly around the waist.

The remainder of the team would then form a bridge with each boy putting his head between the legs of the boy in front of him and gripping him around the thighs as they do in a rugby scrum.

The other team then had to jump on to the bridge, making sure no part of their body or clothing touched the ground. It was important that the first one or two of the jumpers got as far up the bridge of backs as possible, to enable their whole team to get on.

Once all the jumping team were on they had to shout out. 'Bung-the Barrel, Bung-the-Barrel, Bung, Bung, Bung.' After three successful jumps the sides changed round. If, on any of the jumps someone, or someone's clothing touched the ground, the teams changed round immediately. However, if the bridge collapsed, then that jump was taken again.

The game was banned from the school for all time due to a serious injury to Johnny Swift from Single Hill. During one game the bridge collapsed and he suffered a badly broken leg.

Two other games we played were quoits, Shoscombe had won the World Quoit Championship sponsored by the News of the World in nineteen thirty-six, and 'fives', a game loosely related to squash, which we played against the angle of the walls created by Miss Chambers's room and the Managers room. Played by two players, the object was to hit the ball with your hand against the walls in such a way as to make it difficult for your opponent to return it.

The girls played games of their own such as hopscotch and skipping, and one played with two tennis balls called Two Ball. The balls were bounced off the ground and against the wall in such a way that they returned to hand. The deliveries were complicated for the balls would be delivered from both sides of the player, from under each leg and from behind the back until with the sequence over, they would begin it again. Some of the girls perfected their skills to such a high level that it was not unusual to find a great many of us standing watching them all through playtime.

To these games were added those that were played by both girls and boys together, such as French Cricket, Stool-ball, Rounders, Touch and sometimes, but not often, Leap-frog. When the weather kept us inside we played Hunt-the-Thimble, Tippit, How-Green-you-Are, I-Spy and Blindman's Buff.

The one exception that blighted all of our lives was the school dentist. For weeks before he actually arrived and set up his surgery in the chapel hall at Shoscombe, every one of us suffered the stomach sickness his impending visit always brought.

On the day when we actually had to make the journey for treatment, the number of visits we made to the toilet rose to double figures. All treatment, it seemed to us, was carried out as roughly and painfully as possible; almost as though we had unknowingly done something that had upset the dentist and for which he was getting his own back.

*   *   *

EIGHT

The education we received at St. Julian's was much more than the elementary standard deemed sufficient to prepare us for our proper 'station' in life which was either the coal mines or farm labouring for the boys and factory or shop work for the girls. Such schools were required only to teach the three Rs in the classroom, with needlework for the older girls and gardening for the boys. At the age of eleven the girls were taught cookery and the boys woodwork.

Those facts must have been ignored by our teachers, for not only were we taught the basics of reading and writing, we were also introduced to the stories and poetry of Longfellow, Dickens, Barrie, R.L. Stevenson, and Wordsworth and the plays of Shakespeare. Not only did we read 'A Midsummer Night's Dream', each of us taking the part of one of the characters, we later went to the Old Vic Theatre in Bristol where we saw it brought to life on stage.

Arithmetic also went beyond the four principles of add, subtract, divide and multiply, into the land of geometry and algebra.

Alongside the learning we did in school, and very much a part of our overall education, was the learning that we did outside of school. It was given to us by 'teachers' who were experts, and who spoke with the authority and knowledge they had accumulated through the years they had spent 'doing the job' but who, because of their occupations, everyday lives and backgrounds were considered by many of the book 'experts' to have little of consequence or value to offer. Housewives and coal miners, farm labourers and roadsweepers, were the people we learned from.

Though some of them could neither read nor write, they all passed on to us a great awareness of the environment and our responsibilities to it. They also instilled in us a sharing and caring attitude to people, animals and the land itself.

Had it been suggested to them that they were reservoirs of knowledge that would never, could never, be found in books, they would probably have answered, "I dunt know about that. Tis all just a matter o' common sense I d'reckon."

Most of the evacuees who found themselves in the area had come originally from London, so few had ever seen a real cow or horse, pig or sheep, goat, hen or duck. No thought had ever been given to where milk came from. Why should it have been when everyone knew it came from bottles or tins?

We were not, nor could we ever have been, prepared for the reality of life in the countryside. The whinnying of horses and the smoothness of their coats, compared to the coarseness of their manes and tails. The scritch of harness as it moved to the metronomic clop of the horse's hooves accompanying us along the road to adulthood. The abrasiveness of a cow's tongue when it licked our hand. The warm silky feel of goats. The stiff wiriness of pigs. The wind through the trees. The applause of rain on leaves. Bird song.

Holding together the mixture of size, sounds and texture, was a single common thread; the smells of the countryside, most of them pleasing to the senses. Manure, when dung heaps were opened and their contents loaded onto carts and taken to the fields where it was spread to ensure good crops.

The smell of freshly cut grass and curing hay. The dairy at milking time. Bonfires at different times of the year. Hot tar. The countryside after rain. Stables.

We learned the local names for some of the birds we saw. The wren, which was used as an emblem on the 'tail' side of a farthing was known locally as a 'scutty'. Yellowhammers were called 'writing larks' because, we were told, if we looked at their eggs carefully we would find our initials 'written' on them. A wood pigeon was know as a 'quist'.

Another bit of countryside ingenuity we learned was how to obtain the skeletons of small animals and birds. When we found something dead that interested us, we would take it to the nearest ants nest and lay the carcass on it. Several days later all that would be left were the bones which we would lift carefully and take home, where they would be added to the other treasures we had accumulated.

Sometimes we learned things about the countryside in a completely unexpected manner. Such an event took place one morning on our way to school.

Going down Rag Hill, Frank and I stopped to look at an ants nest in the bank. Our interest that day was caused not so much by the level of activity taking place, but the sight of the ants carrying white tube-shaped objects, much larger than themselves, away from the nest.

We were so engrossed watching them, that we didn't notice the rest of the group had gone on down the hill until one of the girls called to us in a very bossy voice to "catch up." Absorbed as we were, we did not immediately comply with her order.

Our lack of instant obedience brought her marching back up the hill where, grabbing me by the arms she gave me a good shaking which was followed by a push-start down the hill. Then turning to Frank, she gave him such a hard wallop that he was knocked off his feet and into the bank.

His reaction was swift and deadly accurate. Jumping to his feet he grabbed a handful of the ants' nest and flung it at her, hitting her smack in the chest. While much of it fell on the ground, some of it found its way inside her blouse.

That was when we learned that ants had a painful bite. How painful we didn't hang around to find out, for while she began performing the dance of 'The Ants and the Maiden', we made ourselves scarce. That was the only morning I remember Frank and I arriving at school by ourselves and not as part of the group.

*   *   *

One evening after tea, I left the bungalow with Uncle Gilb and together we followed the path at the back of the bungalow that ran between the garden hedge and the trees, to a part of the batch I had not visited before.

We walked for some distance before turning off the path and pushing through ferns that grew higher than my head, where we began climbing up the side of the batch. Reaching a place he had chosen beforehand, we sat down behind a large elder bush with a caution from him that I wasn't to move or make a sound no matter what I saw or heard.

It was a pleasantly warm evening with the sun appearing to be almost resting on the tops of the trees. Birds flying near us called to each other that the day would soon be over. From a tree farther up the batch, the sound of a woodpecker rapping on a tree punctured the evening air as it worked to gain entry to the grub-laden larder that waited beneath the bark.

Sitting there, noises that generally went unnoticed were very clear. Birds moving about in the trees. The rustlings of small animals scuttling through the undergrowth. The sighs of the leaves as breezes, making their journey into the coming night, brushed gently against them, whispering the secrets of the day just ending.

A magpie landed on a nearby tree and sat watching us, as though unable to make up its mind as to what we were or why we were there. It kept ruffling its feathers making the black and white colours flash in the evening sun, and cocking its head from side to side as if to get us in better perspective. Out across the field toward Woodborough Pond, a kestrel hovered on outstretched wings searching the ground below for its last meal of the day. Flocks of starlings began splashing their ink blob bodies across the reddening paper of evening's sky, before all wheeling and coming together to roost for the night in the trees.

Below them other birds were making their own journeys home, while in the fields the familiar rabbits were beginning to leave the dark, warm, safety of burrows and begin feeding. How many would fall prey to foxes or poachers and provide a meal for a hungry family before the night was over? Whenever Auntie was going to skin one she would say, "I reckon we'd better go and take the jacket off Mr Rabbit and pop'n in the oven so he don't catch cold."

As real dusk was approaching, Uncle Gilb touched my arm and directed my gaze to an area across and lower down from where we sat. At first I couldn't see what he was indicating then, not more than fifty feet away, an animal the size of a collie dog but with shorter legs and tail appeared and I was looking at my first live badger.

Slate-grey in colour, it had two broad bands of dark hair running up its white face from its nose across its cheeks and eyes until they joined the dark hair of its back behind its ears. It was a boar, Uncle Gild told me later, checking all was safe before allowing the rest of his family to emerge.

We watched as he moved slowly around the entrance of the sett, sniffing the ground and smelling the air. He seemed to be satisfied that all was well for he sat down and proceeded to scratch and groom himself with the long claws protruding from his toes.

After some ten minutes of grooming, during which he kept up a continual sniffing of the air, he must have given some kind of signal for from the entrance of the sett came five small badgers that were obviously cubs, followed by several larger badgers.

Immediately the young ones began playing in front of the sett, chasing each other and rolling about like children in a playground. A most surprising thing about their play was the fact that they did it in almost total silence.

The boar, as soon as the other animals were outside, set off on his own down the batch and into the tall ferns through which we had come earlier, although not in the same place. As he left, more badgers appeared and began a similar display of ground smelling and air scenting as the first one before they too began their own grooming. Then, while some of the older badgers went off on their own, others remained to supervise the young ones.

We sat watching until it became almost too dark for us to see them then, moving quietly away we came down off the batch onto the path and walked home through the friendly darkness.

Over supper Uncle Gilb told me a lot more about badgers. The best places to look for a sett and how to tell if it was in use. A pile of used bedding outside the entrance. Several trails leading to and from it. One or more dung pits in the area. All these were good signs.

He also explained that if left undisturbed badgers would use the same sett for years. He'd watched the one we'd been to since long before the war.

During the next few weeks we visited the sett regularly, during which time I learned much more about those beautiful shy animals, both by watching them and from Uncle Gilb. Some evenings the lonely call of an owl would float out onto the dark softness of the coming night to be followed, if we were lucky, by a sight of the bird ghosting by on silent wings.

*   *   *

One of the rules mother enforced rigidly was the care of my clothes. The first thing I had to do each day on arriving home from school was change out of my school clothes and into my play ones.

Going into the bedroom one evening I found a boy sitting on a chair at the end of mother's bed. I stood staring at him wondering who he was while at the same time feeling there was something familiar about him, while he just sat staring back. It was when he stood up and walked over to me that I realised who he was.

"You're George!" I said. "You're my brother George."

"So you do recognise me. I thought for a while there that I was going to have to introduce myself to you," he said, while I stood there not believing it was really him.

"Who told you where we lived?" I asked him at last. "How did you get here?"

"With great difficulty," he told me. "I travelled during the night and arrived in Bath early this morning. Then I was sent to another station and put on a train that was going to somewhere called Radstock. That was a mistake. I should have been told to get out at a place called Single Hill."

"What did you do?" I wanted to know.

I had to wait at Radstock for another train to take me back to Single Hill and even when I got there I found I was still miles from this place. Luckily, a man with a horse and cart was coming this way and he gave me a lift."

"Are you going to stay here with us now" I asked him, "or do you have to go away again?"

"I'm home for good," he assured me. "That's why mother sent for me."

From then on the quality of my life increased greatly; not only did I have another boy to play with at home, but one who was also my brother. Despite being a quiet person who rarely spoke and who enjoyed nothing better than to read a book, he always joined in the games we played and the things we did.

Searching for birds nests was a thing I enjoyed doing and so it was not surprising that among the first things I showed him was the 'scutty's' nest I had found in the hedge at the bottom of the garden. From then on we spent hours looking for other nests.

Batch tobogganing was another thing he took to, and in a short time became skilled at guiding the 'toboggan' through the maze of trees and arriving safely at the bottom still in one piece.

Auntie Weeks had a wireless set that I had never paid any attention to until George returned home. Then, because of his interest in it, I began listening in the evenings to reports of the battles being fought. The news, that always began with the newsreader giving the station, the time and his name, led to a guessing game we all played.

"This is the B.B.C. Home Service, here is the nine o' clock news and this is ...... At that point, before the newsreader could say it, we would call out the name of the person who we thought it was. If our guess was correct, joy. If it was wrong well, see if I care. It's a stupid game anyway.

Many times programmes were interrupted with the words "Here is a special announcement" or "Here is a special bulletin." When that happened everyone stopped whatever they were doing or saying at the time to listen in absolute silence until the message was ended.

Some of the broadcasts began with the V for victory sign, DUM-DUM-DUM-DA, DUM-DUM-DUM-DA, being beaten out on a bass drum. That sound also caused everyone to remain breathlessly quiet, until the voice on the wireless told us, "We are now returning you to your interrupted programme."

*   *   *

Late summer, and the hedges were full of blackberries all waiting to be picked and so, like the old lady who went from 'Weep to Wicking', Auntie and I, each of us carrying a bowl, set off. Lesson number one, that blackberries are guarded by sharp thorns which they use to good effect on the fingers of unsuspecting boys, was quickly learned, and the gathering of the blackberries provided us with an enjoyable way to spend some of the late summer afternoons.

The results of the hours spent picking those blackberries were enjoyed through the long cold months of winter in the form of blackberry jam, some of which was used in tarts made on large enamel plates and smaller pies and turnovers which we were sometimes given to eat while they were still hot from the oven.

Snow brought with it not only the message that Christmas was near again, but also the chance for us to enjoy the more universal form of tobogganing. When Uncle Gilb brought out a sledge big enough to seat three riders at the same time, we couldn't wait to try it out.

The run, which was really steep, ran across two long fields separated from each other by a hedge. To get from the first field to the second meant not only steering through a hole in the hedge, but on reaching the hole having to lie right back on the toboggan in order to ensure our heads remained on our bodies and were not left stuck in the hedge feeling unwanted.

The appearance of familiar sights was greatly altered by the heavy falls of snow, and the scene from the bungalow was very different to the one we were used to. The rough patches in the track had all been smoothed off, as had the unevenness of the fields and the tops of the hedges and bushes. The wire of the fences and the bars of the gates could be seen even after dark stretching out like lengths of thick white wool.

It was the trees, standing naked before the ravages of winter, that made the greatest impression on me. The thin twigs at the ends of their branches moving slightly like the fingers of supplicants begging for forgiveness, made me feel sorry for them.

Soon after Christmas came the news that Ted was coming home again, cured of the illness that had almost claimed his life. The next few days were full of excitement and preparations for his return.

The weather on the day that he was to be discharged was far from welcoming. The sun was a pale, watery looking blob, that appeared to make no effort to push aside the early morning mist while the grass and bushes, heavy in dew, stood in bowed misery, instead of sharing the joy we were feeling.

That was the day I rode in a motor car for the first time. Mother had hired a taxi from King's garage at Peasedown and together with Auntie Weeks we set off.

It is difficult to describe the scene that greeted us on our arrival for it seemed that not only were all the nurses and doctors there to see him off, but most of the patients also. As for presents, there can never have been so many heaped on one small boy. Toys, clothes. gifts of money, they seemed to go on without end. But of all the gifts he received that day the best was the title of 'Miracle Baby' the medical staff who had saved his life bestowed on him.

March arrived in its usual ill-tempered, blustery manner, trying to push and boss everyone and everything about. The trees for their part showed they were not prepared to give in to its bullying as their branches struck back in firm resistance to the meddlesome wind that sought to upset and disturb them.

It was also in March that the unbelievable happened when one night as we were getting ready for bed, mother announced we were leaving Auntie Weeks and going to live in Shoscombe. I cannot describe the stunned disbelief and deep hurt I felt when she told us. Leave Auntie Weeks to go and live in some miserable house in Shoscombe. I couldn't take it in.

It took me no time at all to make up my mind that I for one would never leave the bungalow or Auntie Weeks, and there was nothing anyone could say or do that would make me.

*　　*　　*

NINE

The day we moved to Shoscombe the sun, unlike the day that Ted had come home from hospital, was bright and cheerful as it played now-you-see-me, now-you-don't, with the small white clouds that sailed across the sky to the crowing cheers of cockerels and the music of bird song.

The cottage we moved to was owned by a man named Mr Bundy, and stood next door but one to the Apple Tree public house. It was a small cottage with two bedrooms and a box room upstairs, and a parlour and scullery downstairs. Beneath the stairs, which were closed off from the parlour by a door, was a large cupboard that was used as a coal cellar, to which soon would be added the duty of air-raid shelter.

Beside the front door the tall back of a wooden settle formed one side of a passage into the room, to the left of which was the door that led into the scullery. That settle provided the room with extra seating, kept the draughts from the open door off the backs of our legs, and kept the heat from the fire in the living area of the room.

With the exception of the two days when the chimney was being swept, the fire was kept burning for twelve months of the year being used daily for cooking, heating and providing hot water for drinks and bathing. Although mother, like most of the other women, cooked every day, she only baked twice a week when she made most of our bread and cakes; shop bought cakes were a luxury.

She also made tarts and biscuits and my favourite, meat and potato pies. Though made with the usual ingredients it was the gravy that made them so special to me.

Fire heat, as she bent to take out or put into the oven whatever she was baking, always gave her face a rosy glow. I loved the invisible changes that took place inside that oven, for pie or tart, cake or loaf of bread, pale and unappetising looking when put in, would be taken out later a lovely golden brown, their aromas filling the whole house and confirming my belief that only the best and strongest kind of magic could have brought about such change.

One thing she never made was 'Inspiration Pie' a concoction that could only have been dreamed up by one of those very important committees or a chef de cuisine, for who else could have produced a recipe that not only used potatoes as a the filling, but as the crust as well?

Mr Bundy, probably because he was an old man, did not eat very much. What he did eat, however, left us feeling quite sick until we became used to it.

His breakfast always consisted of what he referred to as 'slingers'. The meal was prepared by breaking an egg into a bowl to which was added salt and pepper. Next, several thick slices of bread broken into small pieces would be put in the bowl on top of the egg and covered with boiling water. Once the water had soaked in hot milk was poured over the contents which were then ready to eat.

The meal was always eaten with a lot of oohs and mmms, each mouthful being accompanied with loud sucking sounds similar to those made by a herd of cows walking through deep mud. The final accolade for a meal enjoyed was a brisk rubbing of the stomach that resulted in a very loud, and very disgusting, belch.

His supper was a thick slice of buttered bread and a large chunk of very strong cheese, washed down with a pint of rough cider into which, before he drank it, he would plunge the red-hot poker he had heated in the fire. Like breakfast, that meal also was filled with loud sucking noises.

*   *   *

Although most of the housework was done by mother, we had to make our beds and keep our bedroom tidy. We also had to help prepare the vegetables, take it in turn to lay the table and wash up afterwards, a job I hated, especially when the plates were greasy.

Before the dishes were washed the water was made as soapy as possible to help remove the grease. That was done by making holes in the bottom of a golden syrup tin into which we then put any bits of soap no longer big enough for us to wash ourselves with.

The tin was stood in the bowl used for washing the dishes and boiling water from the kettle poured into it. Then the tin was swished about in the water to make it soapy; it never did though. All that happened was the water turned a cloudy, grey-blue, colour.

On washdays, before leaving for school, we had to make sure that the copper was filled with water, the fire was lit and burning well, and that a supply of fuel was ready to hand. During the school holidays we had to share, George and I the job of turning the handle of the mangle while mother fed the newly washed clothes into it.

As each load of washing was finished and taken from the copper in sparkling cleanliness, thanks to 'Paddy the Wonder Washer' or 'Oxydol' soap powder, another was begun. Once all the boiling was completed, usually late in the afternoon, we had to draw the fire, empty the copper of dirty water and lift the ashes.

*   *   *

Life was not all work. We had plenty of time to play the games that children had played for centuries and some we made up for ourselves.

One that we really enjoyed and called 'rattle-the-stick', involved one of us creeping quietly into the house and then rattling Mr Bundy's walking stick, which hung on the back of the settle when not in use, up and down to make as much noise as we possibly could, then running away before he could catch us.

Down the garden we would race to where the ash heap lay piled against the garden wall. Running up it, we would jump across the small stream that trickled past on the other side, then on up the field where we collapse in a breathless heap, safe from his angrily shaken fist.

George, a master of innovation and good ideas and always ready to try out something new, decided one day that he would change his method of escape and so, while I continued over the wall and up the field, he ran into the privy. Once there he was not content to remain hidden, but had to see what was going on. To do so he had to stand up on the seat where, instead of looking where he was putting his feet, he somehow missed the seat altogether and went straight through the hole to finish up to his knees well and truly 'in it'.

Rescuing himself, no-one was going to help him, he was left standing alone and friendless in the small stream, where he had to wash away all the visual and scented evidence of his miscalculation before anyone would go near him. After that, he stuck to our tried and tested escape route.

Ted, who because he was too young to join in some of our games, spent much of his time visiting the neighbours of whom Mrs Stock, known as 'Stocky' and Mrs Drew at the Apple Tree were his favourites. He came in one day carrying a brown paper bag which he showed to mother.

"What's that you've got?" she asked him.

"Currants," Ted answered.

"Currants?" said mother. "Where did you get currants?"

"I went to see Stocky and she gave them to me," he told her.

"Let me see them," said mother, taking the bag from him and opening it.

To her surprise she found the bag held not currants but rabbit droppings. It turned out to be one of Stocky's little jokes.

*   *   *

Soon after moving to Mr Bundy's cottage, mother bought a wireless set of our own that allowed us to continue listening to the programmes we had enjoyed at Auntie Weeks's. It also gave us a new interest as countries and places which up until then had just been different patches of colour in our atlases at school, became more real.

Country names such as Germany, Poland and Russia, made a noticeable improvement to our geographical knowledge as we went hurrying to our atlases to look them up, each trying to be the first to find them. In addition we were able, after first making sure we would not be arrested and shot as spies, to parade before what we felt sure was a very impressed adult audience, our ability to speak foreign languages.

Cigarette cards was another enjoyable way of learning that was greatly helped by the people in the village who were always adding to our collection. Each card had a picture on the front with a written description on the back and covered subjects as varied as history, science, medicine, geography, famous men and women, places, inventions, animals and birds.

As the war continued, to our list of foreign places such as Egypt, North Africa, Singapore, Japan and Malta, we added the names of some of the men leading the fighting. Alexander, Montgomery, Wavell, and a man named Rommel who, for reasons we could not work out, seemed to spend his time fighting 'desert rats' instead of getting on with the war.

There were some, such as Chittagong and Imphal, that we were doubtful about, especially if we could not find them in our atlases. However, George came up with the answer. The places did not exist. Mr Churchill had told our soldiers to make them up so that the enemy would not know where our army was.

It was not just war news the wireless broadcast. There was a variety of programmes to entertain the listener ranging from classical music and concerts, to comedy and plays, with the daily helping of 'Workers' Playtime' and the twice daily 'Music While you Work'.

Among the programmes were some that became popular with everyone. I.T.M.A. with Tommy Handley, The Happidrome, with Mr Lovejoy, 'Ee if ever a man suffered', Ramsbottom and Enoch 'Ee Mr Lovejoy, I think I'm in love', who ended every show with a tap dance, and Band Waggon, with Richard Murdoch and Arthur Askey.

Some of the shows had a ventriloquist that led Frank to ask if we thought when they were on the wireless and we couldn't see them, they moved their lips? After giving the question serious thought we decided the answer was no. To do so would be cheating.

Paul Temple regularly solved mystery and murder cases in six or eight episode adventures, one episode a week. Saturday Night Theatre introduced us to some first-class plays, while the Robinson Family, and Dick Barton, Special Agent, omnibus edition Saturday, kept us entertained each afternoon and evening, Monday to Friday.

The Man in Black, Valentine Dyall, brought us stories that were guaranteed to send even the bravest to their bed in a state of nervous apprehension with the plea "Don't blow out the candle mum."

Many varied sayings and songs came into vogue due to the war among which the sayings most often used were, 'Put that light out', 'Don't you know there's a war on?' 'It's that man again', and 'Oi! mind my bike'. And while the air-raid sirens rose and fell in competition with Vera Lynn singing about the White Cliffs of Dover, we sang a song that cast grave doubts on the anatomical completeness of Hitler, Goering, Himmler and Goebbels, to the tune of Colonel Bogie.

Wireless sets required two things to make them work; a battery and an accumulator. The battery, depending on how much the wireless was used, lasted between four to six weeks, while the accumulator lasted only a week before needing to be re-charged.

Most families had two accumulators; one in use while the other was being charged either at King's garage at Peasedown, or Maggs Engineering Works at Welton, who collected and delivered. As we had ours charged at the garage it meant a weekly journey to Peasedown, usually on Saturday morning, to leave the empty one and bring back the charged one.

From the beginning those weekly trips brought together, though not in a truly educational way, our minds and bodies with some of the local boys. Every week, five or six of them would be waiting by the tin chapel and as we got near them would, while muttering something that sounded like 'zum more of they evacs', line themselves across the road in a manner that left us in no doubt that there was only one way we were going to get past them. As it was a situation that could be resolved in only one way we were forced to take it. Mind you, we always got to the garage with the empty accumulator and returned with the charged one.

Mother, who was not noted for her forbearance, was always angry when we arrived home our shirts dirty and torn, with buttons missing and stained with blood from nose-bleeds that was not always our own.

Each time we tried to explain to her what had happened all she would say was, "I'm sick and tired of telling you both to stay away from those boys.

*   *   *

TEN

April 25th/26th. The sky over Bath bled its sorrow into the night's blackness as exploding bombs razed buildings and ushered dreams into the nothingness of oblivion.

The first of the Baedecker Raids began around 11.00p.m. and lasted until the 'All Clear' sounded two and a half hours later. During the raid, while we sat in a huddle of silent, fear-filled excitement in the cellar under the stairs Mr Bundy, despite mother's pleas, refused to come away from the window.

"This is my home," he told her, "and none o' thik lot up there is gwanna make I hide in me own home."

And there he remained continually lighting his pipe, the matches flaring in the darkness as though daring the pilots of the planes throbbing overhead to do something about it.

Respite for the city was short-lived for around 5.00a.m. a second raid began, adding greatly to the death, injury, and destruction, that had been done only a few hours earlier.

Daylight, and from the top of the field in front of the cottage, smoke from the fires could be seen resting darkly against a sky that only recently had greeted the arrival of another new Spring.

The third and final raid began just after 1.00a.m. on the morning of Monday the 27th, and continued for two hours. During that time the bombers subjected the people and the city to a non-stop rain of incendiary bombs dropped to add to all the havoc wreaked by the high explosive bombs dropped during the earlier raids.

One good thing that came out of the bombing of Bath was a boy called Johnny Nichols. We became firm friends when he came with his mother to live in the village. He also had an older brother who was serving in the R.A.F.

As a result of the bombings, the local policeman came to school and gave us a talk about things we might find lying in the fields or on the roads that were not to be kicked, picked up or touched in any way, even though they looked familiar.

He showed us some of them and explained that what looked like an ordinary cocoa tin or golden syrup tin, could be a device that was rigged to explode when touched. Balloons, the kind we hung around the house at Christmas and on birthdays, were another possible danger as they may have been treated with poison to kill anyone putting them in their mouth.

We were also warned to be on the alert for people called 'Fifth Columnists' on bikes. If we saw anyone who was acting in a furtive or suspicious manner especially at night, or saw them doing things with torches, such as switching them on and off or waving them about, we were to go and tell someone.

When the lecture was over we had to clap in appreciation of his warnings, despite the fact we had no idea what words like furtive and suspicious meant. As for people called 'Fifth Columnists' well, none of us had a clue what he was on about. What worried us most of all was the fact that just about everyone we knew rode a bicycle, including the policeman.

*   *   *

As well as being a pub, the Apple Tree also had a small counter immediately opposite the front door from where Mr and Mrs Drew sold cigarettes, tobacco, biscuits, crisps, and sweets when they were available. Outside, at the foot of the slope, was a small room that Mr Drew used as a paraffin dispensary and, more importantly, as a store for the empty biscuit tins which he allowed us to search through to collect the pieces of broken biscuits in them while we waited for him to fill our can with paraffin.

One day when I had been sent for paraffin, Mr Drew told me to go up to the store and wait for him. There I went through the empty biscuit tins as I always did then, as he had not arrived by the time I had finished, I decided to help him by filling the can myself.

Placing the measure he used under the pump, I climbed up on to the storage tank and began to work the handle as I had seen him do it. It was when the measure was nearly full that things began to go wrong, for where the paraffin stopped for Mr Drew with me it kept pouring out. Gallons of it continued to gush from the pump and over the sides of the measure, from where it ran down the sides of the tank, across the floor and out through the door onto the large flagstones outside.

When Mr Drew finally arrived it was plain to see he was not at all pleased with my efforts to help. I think his feelings were summed up when he told Mrs Drew that I was without doubt the 'worsomest kid he'd ever known'. "Only time we'm safe from'n is when he's in his bed and fast asleep, and even then you got t'keep both your eyes open."

It didn't stop me going for paraffin, or stop him letting me go through the biscuit tins. What it did stop was me going near the store again on my own.

The Apple Tree was not just a place where we went to buy paraffin and eat

61

broken biscuits. It was also a source of great pleasure to us especially at weekends. Then through the open window of the snug, the click of dominoes and the shussh of metal discs across the shove-ha'penny slate, added their melody as beer glasses tinkled background music to accompany the rise and fall of voices as they performed their Saturday evening concerto of friendship and quiet contentment.

On those evenings we listened to stories of people who had been a part of the village community and some of the things they were thought, or known, to have done. We heard of dogs who had earned places in village history through their rat-catching or poaching abilities. Woven into the general talk, if anyone in authority had been there and cared to listen, was the sure and certain way to end the war and get the country 'back to normal' and on its feet again.

*   *   *

In 1940, Antony Eden had called for civilians to create their own Local Defence Volunteers, later to be renamed the Home Guard. The formation of these local groups allowed the trained regular soldiers, to be sent where they were most needed.

Shoscombe, as elsewhere, formed their own detachment and used the Apple Tree as one of their meeting points. They were commanded by Ian Beauchamp, the son of a local mine-owner, who had the rank of Captain, while Mr Drew held the rank of Lieutenant. Leonard Stock, Herbert Wilton and Stanley Stone were the sergeants, while the remainder held the rank of private.

Training to carry out their duties was done on a regular basis, generally at weekends. As their only weapons consisted of several 12-bore shotguns, the men used broom handles when doing rifle drill, with large knives tied to the ends when doing bayonet practice. However, their fire power was greatly increased the day they received a consignment of one rifle.

The importance of that solitary weapon was made obvious one night by Stan Nineham who was lodging with Mrs Weston and her family. He had been off work all week with a severe bout of flu, so it was a very surprised Mrs Weston who found him in his home-guard uniform ready to go out.

"You'm never goin' out are you Stan?" she asked him.

"I be," he told her. "'tis a training night tonight, and I got to be there."

"I'm sure they wouldn't mind you missing one night. Not after you bin so sick. I dunt think that you'm well enough to be goin' out yet."

"But I got to be there tonight," Stan explained. "'tis my night for the rifle."

"What do you mean, your turn for the rifle? Haven't you all got rifles then?" Mrs Weston wanted to know.

"No we haven't. There's only the one rifle between the lot of us, and tonight

62

tis my turn to have'n. That's why I got to go." And he went.

On another occasion, as rumour swept the country that the Germans had landed on the south coast, the Home Guard was called away to their mustering post at the Apple Tree, from where they would march to man their post at Wellow cemetery. All the men reported except Fred 'Swanee' Swansbury, who was later found to have been 'incapacitated'. After waiting for some time for him to arrive the rest decided they would have to leave without him.

"We can't hang around here all night else the war's gwanna be over afore we d'get there. When he d'get here you tell'n we'm gone on and he's to hurry and catch us up," were the instructions left with Mrs Drew.

Much later, when she had closed up for the night, the door flew open and into the room burst Swanee, 4.10 shotgun at the ready, demanding to know "Where's the b.....s at?"

"Gave me the fright of my life," Mrs Drew said later, "seeing him standing there waving that loaded gun of his about like a fly swat."

* * *

Soon after the raids on Bath we moved from Mr Bundy's house to a house up near the chapel, where we occupied two rooms above the Knowles family. As the rooms were unfurnished mother had to begin buying the furniture we needed, most of which she got from Mr Coles at Double Hill, who had a small second-hand furniture business.

It was left to George and me using an old pram, to walk to Double Hill and collect whatever new item had been bought. The amount of difficulty we had transporting it home depended on what it was. A table or armchair was far easier to handle than a chest of drawers or wardrobe.

Items mother didn't have to buy were dining chairs. She was given on loan until the end of the war, four camp chairs that could be folded and stood against the wall when not in use. As we had only limited space in the two rooms, they proved to be extremely handy.

* * *

To give the local people a night out together and to take their minds off the war for a few short hours, a concert was arranged and held in the Miner's Welfare hut on the recreation field at the top of Barn Hill.

Although some of the acts were equally as good as any we heard on the wireless others brought no such response. Songs, monologues and jokes all brought varying degrees of enjoyment and pleasure. Uncle Gilb's singing of 'Put a bit of Powder on it Father' and 'When Father papered the Parlour', brought the house down, as did several monologues by another man. Some of the other offerings, however, couldn't end quickly enough.

One was a lady who gave the impression of someone about to break down and cry at any moment as she sang a song about the 'Wings of a Dove', while flapping her arms about as if she had every intention of soaring off the stage at any moment.

At school later we all agreed it would have been an act of great kindness to everyone there that night, if her arms had become the wings she obviously longed for so desperately, as it would have enabled her to carry out her unspoken threat and actually flown away.

She was followed by a lady playing the piano for a man who sang a variety of songs including 'Danny Boy', 'Greensleeves' and 'Don't go down the Mine Daddy', a song that had been written by two miners who had worked at Bromley Colliery.

On the way out after the concert was ended, I bumped into Stan Nineham. I had often seen him around the village but until that evening had never spoken to him.

"Thass alright cuzz," he said, when I apologised, "twer as much my fault as thine."

From then on, whenever we met, he called me cuzz. As I had never heard the word before I was left wondering if it was the local word for clumsy. I eventually found out its meaning the day I heard another new word and repeated it to mother.

*   *   *

Billy from next door and I had each made a bow, and after collecting 'arrows' from the hedge, went up the path between Mrs Symes's house and the chapel to practice our archery in the field.

It became apparent after many tries that Billy just did not have the knack, for instead of releasing the end of the arrow against the string, he kept letting go of the end that rested across the bow. Finally, in a fit of frustrated anger, he flung his bow on the ground at the same time shouting the new word several times. As they disappeared into the far corners of the field, I managed to grab one and add it to my growing list of new and untried words.

Lunchtime came and we set off home. Through the kitchen and up the stairs I went to the front room where everything was in a complete mess. Mother had decided to have the walls white-washed, and had managed to get Stan to do them for her. As I went into the room she was asking him if he would like a cup of tea.

"Ah! That would be lovely," Stan assured her.

"Be a good boy and put the kettle on," she said, turning to me.

It seems that there are times in our lives when no matter how new a word is, or how little we understand its meaning, we have the ability of being able to use it with the maximum impact at the most appropriate time, and in the most engaging manner. That 'new' word was no different.

Although I had done absolutely no practice I still managed that first time of using it, to do so with an aplomb that would have left far more experienced users, had any been present, green with envy. As it was, it left mother white-faced with shock and Stan gasping in what I thought was silent admiration.

"If you want a cup of tea," I told her, "You can put the ..... kettle on yourself."

Saying nothing, she went to the fire and pushed the trivet on which the kettle sat over the flames. When the water had boiled, she made the tea and carried it over to the table. Sitting down eating our lunch, she asked me where I had heard the word.

"Billy said it this morning when he was angry," I told her.

"And where did he hear it?" she wanted to know.

"I have no idea," I answered.

"Well that's the last time you play with him," she told me. "You're not to go near him again. Ever. And I never want to hear you say that word again."

"But he's my friend and ..." I began.

"No he isn't," mother interrupted. "Anyone who uses words like that is nobody's friend."

Further protests got me nowhere. Mother never laid down the law without meaning what she said, and nothing would make her change her mind.

Later, when she had gone downstairs to visit Mrs Knowles, Stan, who was carrying on with the walls, stopped working and came and sat down next to me.

"What made thee go and do a daft thing like that?" he asked me. "If I'd said that to my mother she'd have bumped I that hard I shouldn't have known which day of the week 'twer. You should think yourself lucky you didn't get a good hiding."

"A good hiding. For saying a word I didn't know I wasn't supposed to say?" I asked him.

"But you d'know you'd better not say'n again dunt thee?"

"I do now," I told him. "But what I don't understand is why all the fuss about a word. Why is it alright to say some words but not others? How do we know which is which?"

"I can't tell thee what the answer to that is," he told me, "It be just one o' they things. Mostly the words we d'use all the time be alright. Then there's the ones what d'get'm hoppin' about a bit and can get thee into a hatful of trouble if you d'say them. I dunt know who 'tis do decide which is which."

"What about cuzz then?" I asked. "Is it alright for you to call me that?"

"Course 'tis, else I wouldn' call thee it, would I?"

"But what does it mean?" I wanted to know.

"What that d'mean is that you and I be cousins. Cuzz be just another way of saying it."

I stared at him to see if he was having a joke with me, but hoping at the same time that he wasn't for I liked him a lot.

"Cousins?" I said finally. "What real cousins?"

"Well I dunt know for any other kind," he said. "We'm what they d'call country cousins and they be the best kind."

*　　*　　*

That incident, though never mentioned again, was not the only shock mother received during the time we lived in those two rooms. One we gave her a few days before Christmas, turned out not to be the present we had intended. She had gone to Peasedown to do some shopping when George came up with a great way to help her while she was out. We would scrub the floor.

Getting all the things ready, we poured the hot water from the kettle into the bucket and began. While George did the scrubbing, I came behind mopping up. Our timing was spot on for just as we finished mother arrived home. We heard her talking to Mrs Knowles then hurrying up the stairs, where we waited with wide smiles on our faces.

"What on earth have you two been up to?" she wanted to know as she stood in the doorway of the room with a ready-to-cry look on her face.

"We've scrubbed the floor for you," we told her. "We knew you would be tired when you came home, so we thought that we would help you."

"Scrubbed the floor," mother echoed. "Flooded would be more like it. The water has gone right through into the room downstairs. Mrs Knowles's furniture is getting soaked."

Far from helping her, we had added to her workload and that of Mrs Knowles as well. Far into the night they worked to repair the damage our help had done.

Another incident that could have had very serious, even fatal, results, involved the fire. The coal mother bought had to be supplemented with wood chumps bought from the sawmill at Braysdown pit, some of which we chopped up for kindling.

Sometimes, when the fire was not drawing very well, or the kindling or coal was damp, we would put a pieces of candle among the sticks to help them burn. A sheet of newspaper held in front of the fire to cause a better draught was also used.

One day I went into the house to find George kneeling in front of the fire in a very bad humour, trying to light it.

"Hold a sheet of paper in front of it," I told him.

"I've already done that, and I've tried the candles," he added, before I could suggest it. "It'll just not burn."

"I know what might do it," I said. "Hang on for a minute."

I went back downstairs to the wash-house and filled a milk bottle with paraffin. I had seen it used several times on fires that showed a reluctance to burn, and saw no reason why it should not work for us.

Back upstairs I poured it onto the fire. Immediately clouds of thick smoke began to rise up into which I threw a lighted match with spectacular results, for not only did the paraffin explode into action and set fire to the chimney, the flames also shot out into the room setting fire to mother's armchair.

If Mr Knowles, a fireman with the Bath Fire Brigade, had not been at home that day, the entire house would have burned to the ground. He had it under control in a very short time and with the help of some of the neighbours, took the burned armchair out to the garden then set about tidying the room. The walls that Stan had so recently white-washed, all had to be washed down and redone.

*   *   *

ELEVEN

We **knew that Spring** was near again when the rooks returning to the rookeries, began calling out their raucous greetings to other well-known neighbours. For days we watched them fly in to nesting places high in the tops of the trees, carrying the twigs with which they would build there untidy nests. Often one of the more enterprising would wait their chance to steal twigs from other nests, an act that resulted in a long and loud disagreement between robber and robbed.

The smaller birds, once their singing and noisy showing off had successfully attracted a mate, went about the task of building their own nests in the hedges and bushes in a much quieter manner. As soon as the noisy bustle of courtship was over, the countryside returned to a more peaceful and gentle life-style.

From the very outset life in the countryside fascinated me and with few exceptions, I loved everything it had to offer. There were times though when Nature played tricks on us so that what our eyes told us was one thing, turned out to be something totally different when touched.

A good example of this occurred the day I was sitting on our garden wall with Eileen Marsh who lived next door, when a movement on top of the wall across the road from where we sat caught my attention. Seeing the speckled breast I knew it was a thrush going to its nest. Jumping down, I went across the road to the gate that gave access to the field behind and climbed up it on to the wall, then walked carefully along to the place where I had seen the movement.

Looking down between the stones I saw it sitting quietly, its speckled breast rising and falling in time to its breathing. Carefully stretching my arm down I gently picked it up and lifted it out of the wall.

It was only then that my skill at bird recognition proved to be seriously deficient, for instead of a thrush I found in my hand the biggest, ugliest, toad that I had ever seen. So great was my shock, that I threw it away from me with such force that it caused me to overbalance and fall back into a large, and very unfriendly, bed of nettles.

I learned two important lessons that day. One, not only thrushes had speckled breasts and two, that beds of stinging nettles are vastly inferior to real beds.

Our move to Shoscombe did not stop me going back to see Auntie Weeks at every opportunity or having my tea at Frank's castle. Many times, when disobeying mother's instructions that I was not to go, I smuggled my play clothes out of the house and either took them to school with me or hid them to collect later.

At Frank's, his mother always gave us our tea before she would allow us to leave and begin carrying out the things we had planned. Sometimes we climbed up Small Batch to collect pieces of rock that held the imprint of leaves and ferns that had grown when the area was part of a tropical swamp.

Other times we would sit watching the wheels at the pit head speed round as the cages were lowered and raised until they began slowly slowing, slowing, slowing, until they stopped then, with a slight movement of the wheels in the opposite direction, the cages came to rest. That was followed by the dull thumps of empty tubs displacing the full ones as they were loaded into the cage to begin their own journey down into the pit.

One evening we were sitting listening to George Formby's latest record, when we were interrupted by a commotion in the lane outside. Following Mrs Weston, who had gone to see what was happening, we found Margaret and another girl called Jean Beer who was holding a bloodstained handkerchief to her face.

Another woman who had also gone to investigate turned to Mrs Weston and called, "'tis alright. No harm bin done. 'tis just one of they accidents what d'happen."

"Well what did happen?" Frank's mother asked, looking at the handkerchief getting redder and redder.

"Oh, the two of them were just playin' around," the woman explained. "Your Margaret were swinging her nose round her head and went and accidently hit Jean in the schoolbag wi' it."

*   *   *

When for any number of reasons I couldn't get to Frank's, Johnny and I played with another boy named Lennie Giles who, with two other evacuee brothers called North, was billeted with Mr and Mrs Allen who lived in the Barracks at the other end of the village.

Once, when all three of us were up on the rec. playing some game or other, Johnny pointed to a tower standing guard-like on the horizon against the afternoon sky.

"How far d'you think it is from here to that tower?" he asked us.

We sat for a while looking at it through squinted eyes, then Lennie said, "About sixty miles."

"Shall we go over there and see what it's like?" Johnny said.

"Not now," answered Lennie. "If we go now I'll be late for home and that will mean trouble for me."

"When shall we go then?" I asked him. "Tomorrow?"

"We can't just go like that," Lennie told us. "We'll have to plan it properly. What if we met some Germans?"

"We'll take catapults," Johnny said. "I'll bet they'd soon run or surrender when they saw us taking aim at them."

Lennie, however, was not prepared to go until everything was properly organised. During the next few weeks more plans were made and rejected than all those needed for the D-Day landings. In the end we never did get to the tower. I think the war was over before we could finally agree.

*   *   *

My favourite outdoor pastime was catching grasshoppers, a pursuit requiring patience, a quick eye and an even quicker hand, a jam jar with grass in it for food, a piece of paper with holes in it and an elastic band. The jar was to hold them, the piece of paper was to stop them escaping and allow them to breath, and the elastic band was to secure the paper.

I had to keep them hidden from mother who always told me off for bringing those overgrown fleas into the house. It was the same with the tadpoles I collected with Frank from the pit pond at Braysdown. She wasn't too bad when they were just tadpoles swimming about in the jar, but as soon as they became small frogs, out of the house they had to go.

One night while she was downstairs visiting Mrs Knowles, I took my grasshoppers to bed with me to study them. I became so engrossed watching them that it was only when I heard mother saying goodnight and the sound of her coming upstairs, that I was alerted to the approaching danger.

Not having enough time to put them back in their hiding place, I put the jar down under the bedclothes and made out I was asleep. Unfortunately the lid came off the jar so that when mother came in to straighten the bedclothes, as she always did before going to her own bed, it was to find the grasshoppers jumping about all over the place when she pulled back the blankets.

The scream she let out must have been heard in Bristol. It certainly got my undivided attention as it brought me upright in the bed, to be met by more screamed words punctuated with hard slaps. I dodged as many as I could while trying to rescue my grasshoppers and get them back into the safety of the jar. However, once the rescue had been completed, mother took the jar and its contents and hurled them out of the window.

I could not understand how she could do such a thing for, along with most of the other grown-ups, she had always taught us to be kind to animals. Advice that had been reinforced by hymns such as 'All Things Bright and Beautiful' that we sang in school and at Sunday School in the chapel hall.

I didn't say it out loud but I knew God was not going to be pleased when He found out. But just in case He didn't, I made sure that future collections always remained well hidden.

*　　*　　*

The present of a magic lantern and sets of slides given to me by a neighbour, led to my first venture into the world of finance. Each set of slides, made of glass, had a series of pictures on them that told a story. A number on each of the slides gave the order in which they were to be loaded into the frame.

The frame into which the slides were placed was mounted on a revolving base, allowing it to move round in a circular manner. In the centre, a candle or small paraffin lamp was placed to light up the slides for viewing. As it revolved metal strips interrupted the light, making the pictures appear animated.

Billy, who I still played with despite mother's warning, came into the wash-house one day as I was loading some of the slides into the frame.

"Wass got there then?" he wanted to know.

"Magic lantern slides," I told him.

"Let's have a look," he said, picking one up and holding it up to the light to see the pictures on it. "They'm pretty good," he said. "wass gwanna do wi'em?"

"Watch them once I've got them in the frame."

Once that was done I lit the piece of candle, and we sat watching the flickering pictures as the frame revolved.

"I reckon we could make some money out of they slides," he said.

"How?" I asked him.

"We could have picture shows and charge everyone a penny to watch them."

Together we arranged the first showing of the slides to the general public. At first things went very well and the pennies, which we shared equally, gave our money-boxes a satisfyingly heavy feel. The venture didn't last long or make us rich, for after seeing the same slides half a dozen times interest in them died, and our venture slid quietly into obscurity.

It wasn't long before another, although not so easy, way of increasing the contents of my money-box presented itself. The miners received two hundredweight of concessionary coal each week, that was delivered in six hundredweight loads by horse and cart, every three weeks.

Helping the miner or his wife to shift the coal from the roadway into the cellar earned me sixpence each time, though mother was not happy at the filthy state I got into.

*　　*　　*

On a frosty night, as the year moved back into Autumn, I went with mother to enquire about the tenancy of a cottage that had become vacant at Shoscombe Bottom. In the bright light of the moon, the cottages stared at us from blackout covered windows as we passed, their roofs silver-sheeted beneath an icy cloak of frost.

Walking across the cinder path, the bushes that appeared so friendly during the day became frightening. Their branches, looking in the moonlight like skeletons' fingers, snatched at our hair and faces as we passed, making me glad that I was not making the journey on my own.

Arriving at the house she was looking for mother explained to Mr Howell, who had answered her knock, that she had come to enquire about the empty cottage.

Taking us into the scullery he went back into the house, returning a few minutes later carrying a candle lantern and accompanied by a dog. With the dog walking quietly at his heels, he led us out of the scullery and down a flag-stoned path to the cottage where, leaving his dog in my nervous company he showed mother round. Back downstairs they came to an agreement suitable to both of them and after paying him the first week's rent, the cottage was ours.

*　　*　　*

TWELVE

The day we moved to the cottage was sunny but very cold. The heavy things we shifted on the pram; the lighter items we carried in boxes and suitcases.

The cottage, the middle one of three, was small, having only a living-room and cellar downstairs, and a bedroom and landing box-room above. In the living-room was the only fire in the cottage where mother cooked and baked and in front of which, in a large tin bath, we all received our Friday night scrubbing.

Daily washes were done in an enamel basin placed on the table, and were always accompanied by bubble blowing. Soaping our hands we would make a circle with our thumb and finger, across which a soapy film would form. By blowing gently on the film it was possible to create some quite large bubbles which floated gently downward to disappear in an explosion of silence when they reached the floor. Sometimes they would burst close to our faces, causing us to jerk our heads back in response to stinging eyes.

The cottage not only brought us the pleasure of having a home of our own again for the first time since we had been evacuated at the beginning of the war, but a garden also that had not one but two plots; one in front of the cottage and the other between the two stables belonging to Mr Howell.

From the front door of the cottage the path led to a gate set in the hedge. On the other side of the hedge lay a drummy road that had once been used by horses towing barges of coal along the defunct Somerset Coal Canal, part of which had occupied what was now the front garden of the cottages.

At the bottom of the slope on the other side of the drummy road where the ground levelled out, were several hens' houses belonging to Mr Craddock, who lived in the house on the other side of Mr Howell. He also kept ducks and calves, while up on the level at the end of his garden was a cow shed and two pig sties.

At the far side of the flat ground stood the embankment that supported what had originally been the S and D, but was then the L.M.S., railway line, that began at Bath Green Park and ran all the way to Bournemouth. Every time a train was heard, we would go rushing up the garden and wave to the servicemen and women packed into it, travelling to and from their theatres of war.

I loved all of the trains, especially those whose drivers returned our waves with loud calls on the engine's whistle. Of them all, my favourite was the Pines Express which every day thundered past at ten minutes to twelve.

Sometimes, when the trains passed at night, reflections from the firebox, as more coal was fed into the fire, would momentarily light up the darkness with a sudden smash of angry heat. On the days and nights when thick fog and mist denied us the chance to see them, the explosions of fog signals set off by the trains assured us that they were still there.

To the right of our garden gate in Mr Howell's front garden stood a pigeon loft and flight. The floor of the loft was raised some two feet off the ground to allow air to circulate and keep the floor dry. It also gave us a clear view of the rats that moved about underneath the loft, attracted there by the pigeons.

To the left in the cottage next door, at the foot of a some stone steps, lived Mr and Mrs Wallace and their family, Doug, Frank, Sid, Fred, Joyce and May. As we already knew them from school, Fred was in the same class as me, we did not have to go through the How-do-you-do, I'm your new neighbour process.

Beyond their cottage the main garden spread away until it reached the hedge that separated it from Mr Horler's. A large Tom Putt apple tree dominated the top of the garden beneath which, separated by a workshop, stood two hens' houses and their runs.

Not only did we have a garden of our own again, we also had our own privy. One of a block of two, it stood at the bottom of the garden between the stable dung heap and a small stream. The next door one was used by the Wallace family.

The privies had been built in that position to make use of the small stream that ran behind them which, it was hoped, would flush them out and carry away the effluent. It proved to be a hope that was doomed to failure, for to clean them out properly and keep them that way, required several hours work once a week.

First, buckets were filled with water at the standpipe in the road, to which plenty of Jeyes disinfectant and strong soda was added, then carried to the privy where it was poured into the pan and left to permeate down through the contents. Next, long-handled wooden spades were employed to push the effluent toward the outlet then more water, with a good measure of bleach added to it, was poured into the pan to flush the contents out through the discharge hole and into the stream.

Once that was done, the seat was given a thorough scrubbing. Twice a year the walls were swept down and white-washed and the door painted.

At the roadside edge of the garden in front of the privies was a large stable built from corrugated sheets of tin, in which the horse was kept during the winter months. A smaller, stone-built stable stood beside the gate that gave access to the front of the cottages.

On our way to school one morning soon after moving to the cottage, we stopped as we were passing the big stable to watch Mr Howell harnessing his horse. As he led it out of the stable we saw to our surprise that it was Kit, the one-eyed horse that was such a favourite with all the children who used the cinder path on their way to school.

We stood watching him as he backed her into the cart and hitched her up. Only when he was ready to lead her out of the stable yard did he speak to us.

"Wass reckon you two's gawpin' at then?" he asked.

"Is that your horse?" we asked him

He stood looking at us.

"Wass mean is it my hoss? Course tis my hoss. What kind of daft question is that?"

"Do you have a grey pony as well?" George asked him.

"Wass that got t'do wi' you?"

"We just wondered, that's all," was our lame reply.

"Well I wouldn' stand about there wonderin' and gawpin' if I were you," he told us. "You'd best get on up the hill to school. You'll be in for it if you'm late."

That day I could hardly wait for the morning to finish. When lunchtime finally crawled into school I ran all the way to the stable to find, to my great disappointment, Mr Howell had not returned from work.

That evening I saw him pass our window on his way down the garden. Quickly finishing my house jobs, I followed and found him in the stable getting ready to clean it out.

"You back again?" he said. "Wass want this time?"

"I came to watch you," I told him.

"Came to watch I what?"

"Whatever it is you're going to do."

"Well I'm gwanna work, and I dunt need anybody watchin' I do that," he informed me. "You'd better get on back up home in case your mother d'need thee."

"Can't I help you?" I asked him.

"Help I? Wass reckon thou could'st do to help I then?"

"I don't know," I replied. "You'll have to tell me."

He stood looking at me for a while then, "Hast thou ever cleaned out a stable?"

When I told him no, he handed me a fork with curved tines."Take that," he told me, "and draw all that dirty straw and manure into a pile and put it outside on the heap."

Doing as he told me I soon had most of it done. It was when it came to cleaning behind Kit's heels that the problem of how to get at it and at the same time keep myself safe arose, for she looked close up in the stable to be at least twice the size she appeared when she was in the field safely behind a barbed wire fence.

"Dunt stand there just lookin' at it," said Mr Howell, "get on wi' it. Tidn't gwanna move itself."

"How am I going to get it out when she's standing all over it?" I asked him.

"She'll move if you d'tell her to," he told me.

"How do I do that? She wont know what I'm saying will she?"

"Course she'll know what you'm sayin'. Wass think she's daft? Just tell her to stand up."

"Would you stand up?" I asked her, feeling really stupid. "Please." My request went completely unrewarded.

"She isn't moving," I said.

"Well tell her again and give her a slap on the rump."

Seeing my hesitation, he stepped past me and gave her a slap at the same time telling her to "stand up." Immediately she stepped forward, allowing me to drag the remainder of the soiled straw into a pile and carry it out to the dung heap.

"You'm gwanna have to do a lot better than that if you d'want to help I," he told me. "You can't come down here and stand about all day when there's work to be done. You got to make sure she d'do what you d'tell her. You'm like that wi' she, wass gwanna be like if I d'want thee to clean out the pony's stable. If you can't do the work because you'm frightened, then tidn't any use for you to come down here asking if you can help I. You'd be better off bidin' up the house helpin' your mother."

The threat of not being allowed back to the stable gave me all the incentive I needed to hide, if not lose, the fear I had of the horse at that time. The next day at the stable, while Mr Howell was through the back in the tack room, I took the fork without waiting to be told and then, with my heart beating faster than usual, I gave Kit a slap and told her in a squeaky voice to "Stand up." Without hesitation she did so.

From then on my confidence grew, and the task of mucking out became one of my favourite jobs. In a surprisingly short time, I found I could go to the stable on my own and work, knowing that Kit would do me no harm.

She turned out to be the most gentle and even-tempered of horses. No matter what she was asked to do, she did with no sign of bad temper or reluctance. She also enjoyed company and was forever snuffling at the pockets of my coat for any titbit I may have brought her.

Joey, the pony, was altogether different. In the field he was the most unfriendly animal in the area; in the stable he was evil. The position of his stall meant that he stood hind on to the door, so that to get into the stable meant having to pass his heels which he was always ready to let you feel. I don't think I went into his stable more than half a dozen times when he was there.

As the days passed, in addition to mucking out I was also allowed to help feed and water her and with harnessing her for work. It was then that Kit showed that in addition to being gentle, she was also a clever animal, especially when it came to getting the heavy work collar on her which, because of its shape, had to be put on upside down then turned around once it was over her head.

Being too heavy for me to lift I could think of no way to put it on her until Kit, by lowering her head, allowed me to get it over her ears. Then, by raising her head, the collar slid down her neck, coming to rest against her huge shoulders where, by climbing up onto the manger, I was able to turn it around to its correct position.

*　　*　　*

School continued to be a source of joy and pleasure. With the coming of the cold weather buckets of water that were poured onto the back playground each day before we went home in the afternoon froze overnight, so that when we arrived at school the next morning we had a ready-made slide to enjoy. Inside the school Mr Gill, the caretaker, had the fires in all the classrooms blazing warmly in front of which we placed our cups or enamel mugs full of milk to heat while we were at our lessons.

At playtime we would add either cocoa powder or ovaltine mixed with sugar to the milk and enjoy a hot drink. At lunchtime, Frank and I would swap some of our sandwiches with each other. There were no cooked school dinners.

An unexpected addition to the variety of our lives was George's dreams. On one occasion he brought the entire house awake as he yelled "They've got me, they've got me." Mother arriving at a rush, found that in his sleep his feet had gone between the bars at the end of the bed and he couldn't get them free.

Another time I was woken by him asking in a quiet voice "Are you awake?"

"I am now." I told him, "What do you want?"

"There's a little man sitting on the end of the bed," he whispered.

"Yeah, I know," I answered, making ready to go back to sleep.

"There is," he insisted, "You take a look."

Doing as he told me, anything for peace, I looked down at the foot of the bed and saw, sitting on the top rail, a little man. The sight of him brought me upright, causing him to move also. As he did we saw that the small man was in fact a large mouse.

*   *   *

The year, still punctuated with war news, moved almost unnoticed through Christmas and the New Year toward Spring. Snowdrops and daffodils brought some relief from Winter's dirty drabness and sometimes, even on days that were still very cold, the pointing fingers of noontime's lengthening shadows painting black shapes on the ground, signalled to us that milder and warmer weather was on the way.

In Spring heavy morning dew made everything, especially the spiders' webs strung in the hedges, glisten like pieces of glass. On those mornings on our way to school, we would break thin green twigs from the hedges and bend them into loops which we then used to lift the webs from the hedge to make 'windows'. We found that if we tied the ends of the twigs together and put the 'window' in a safe place, the dew would dry off and leave the web suspended across the loop allowing us to study it.

Two other skills we learned on our way to school was how to make a whistle with a blade of grass and leaf-popping. To pop a leaf, you first made a circle with the thumb and forefinger of one hand, across which a leaf was placed. Then, holding the other hand flat you brought it down as sharply as you could, forcing the air against the leaf and causing it to burst through with a loud and very rewarding 'pop'.

Grass whistles were made by placing a blade of grass lengthwise between your thumbs and blowing across it. While pleasantly satisfying once the intricacies had been mastered, those whistles could, and often did, give sore reminders in the form of cut tongues and lips, that most things in life had to be learned at some cost to the pupil.

THIRTEEN

As the weather grew warmer the time to begin gardening again arrived. The garden at school had been divided into plots each worked by a leader, always one of the older boys, with one or two of the younger boys as helpers. Frank and I were put in the charge of his older brother Bern.

Once we had dug the ground and prepared the seed bed, the seeds were handed out. One of the packets Bern was given held French beans, something neither Frank nor I had ever seen before.

It was obvious to us, therefore, that they would have to be investigated before we planted them and so, while Bern was showing us how to make the trench in which they would be sown, Frank and I ate them. The uproar that followed could not possibly have been worse had we committed murder.

On our way to school one day, Lennie told us he was going to start a garden of his own.

"Where?" we asked him.

"Where that tree blew down in the field across from Mr Bending's house," he told us.

"Where will you get the seeds?" was our next question.

"I've already got these," showing us a packet of beetroot seeds. "Mr Allen gave them to me. And the man next door has promised me some carrot and lettuce seeds."

When it had blown down, the tree's root pulling out of the ground had created a hollow. It was in the hollow that Lennie made his garden. He borrowed a spade and managed, through the kindness of the neighbours, to get radish and turnip seeds to go with the others which he tended with great care. His reward was a crop of vegetables that was equal to any grown that year in the gardens of the village.

*   *   *

The summer holiday arrived bringing with it two of the year's important events. The first was the school sports and fancy dress parade that was held every year on the rec at the top of Barn Hill.

Success in each age group of the fancy dress was rewarded with the sum of sixpence, with threepence for second place and a penny for third. The races, also run by age, carried with them the same monetary reward.

The party afterwards was the perfect way to end a happy day that was made more so by the cheerfulness of the village ladies who kept our plates loaded and our cups filled. They worked long and hard to make sure that everything went well for us.

The second, the combined Flower and Pet Show, came several weeks later when the women from the surrounding area competed with one another for prizes in baking, cooking, home-made jam, home-made wine, needlework and knitting, while the men vied for the prizes and cups for the best vegetables, fruit and flowers.

There were also classes for the children to show their skills at baking and handicraft. One year, Audrey Blacker made some cakes that won first prize. Her pleasure was, however, dimmed somewhat by Mr White who seemed reluctant to accept that the rich yellow colour of the cakes had come naturally from the yolks of the eggs she had used, and suggested that she had 'added' something to her mixture. She hadn't, but it did spoil for her what should have been a happy and successful day.

While the produce side of the show was well represented, the most important feature, as far as we were concerned, was the prizes won by our pets. Cats, dogs, rabbits, guinea pigs, all found themselves at school in wire cages hired for the day, where they were judged by Mr Gill the school caretaker.

Once the excitement of your pet's success had sunk in; once you had accepted that the card that you held in your hand was proof that your pet was at least third best in the world, you could begin to enjoy the other attractions that always put in an appearance at the show. Hoopla, Lucky Dip, White Elephant stall and raffles, all came together to make it an enjoyable and pleasant afternoon.

*　　*　　*

Soon after the start of the summer holiday Mr Howell, who by then we were calling Uncle Hube, offered mother the job of housekeeper and we moved from our cottage into his house next door.

Downstairs there were two rooms. The large one in which we lived and a best room, into which we were only allowed on special occasions such as Christmas and Easter.

Opposite the door into the main room, an open staircase ran up beside the outside wall leading to three bedrooms and a fair sized boxroom. Being a far larger house meant George and I had a bedroom that was big enough for two beds, a chest of drawers, a large washstand, complete with bowl and jug, and a large wardrobe.

To the right of the stairs on a shelf above the door that led to the lower cellar. sat two glass-fronted display cases. In one a barn owl, a mouse that it would never feed on firmly held in one taloned foot, looked through eyes of brown glass at a world it had once lived in, been part of. The haunting sadness of its call forever silent, its wing-beat now forever still.

In the other a beautiful jay showed off its white and blue capped head and wing tips, its head cocked and turned to one side as if to see better what was causing the disturbance to its now eternal peace.

Their Universe compressed into the last space they would occupy or need, while beside them a venerable old grandfather clock swung its large brass pendulum, ticking both them and us forward on our journey into eternity.

Although we knew that they were no longer alive it was often difficult to accept for their eyes, especially in the flickering light of the fire and candles, seemed to follow every movement we made.

Beside the door into the room was a tall wooden settle like the one in Mr Bundy's house. Between the settle and the window that looked out onto the garden, was a large range, on either side of which was an oven. From a long iron bar above the fire hung large hooks that had originally been used to smoke hams and hang kettles to boil.

In front of the range stood a big table, beside which sat the large wooden armchair used only by Uncle Hube. We sat on the smaller, straight-backed variety or the settle.

The size of the house, while much better as far as space was concerned, also had its detractions, for not only did the jobs we had to do inside the house increase in number, they also took far longer to complete.

The floor was constructed from large flagstones and oh! how we came to hate those huge inanimate objects. They had to be scrubbed twice a week with water liberally laced with soda. Sore on the hands in summer, in winter it was agony. The range was almost as bad. Every Saturday, either George or I had to give it the Zebo treatment. It wasn't good enough to make it shine; it had to sparkle.

However, despite the pain of floor scrubbing and the aching arms from range polishing, the most loathesome job of all was teasing out flock. This was done during Spring-cleaning, when mother took all the mattresses and pillows off the beds and tipped the contents onto a clean sheet spread on the floor.

The following two or three hours would be spent sneezing and teasing the lumps out of the flock, while mother boiled all the mattress and pillow covers. Once dry, the sneezing began all over again as we worked to refill them.

*   *   *

It was during that holiday I began going out on the cart with Uncle Hube. Getting up at five o' clock in the morning guaranteed the excitement I had felt the previous night was more than a little muted, but once the sleep had gone from my eyes it was worth it.

Together through the early morning stillness, we walked up across Sileton's to the top field to collect Kit. Back at the stable it was my job to fetch water for her while Uncle Hube filled the rack with hay.

Once she was settled we left to have our own breakfast before leaving for Writhlington pit at half past six to load the first delivery of the day. Five deliveries would be made before we returned home where, after a bath in front of the fire, we sat down to the meal mother had waiting for us.

The people we delivered to were a mixture of nice, friendly and nasty. The teeth of many of them were so yellowed with age they looked like the keyboard of a piano whose rhythm was broken by gaps that resembled black eyes. Others had no teeth at all, which gave their faces the look of collapsed concertinas.

Some of the women had the habit of folding their arms beneath their large bosoms as though to reinforce an argument that had not yet begun. It was an action that always seemed to me to be much more threatening than if they had put up their fists.

At most of the houses we were offered tea or lemonade. One exception was a woman with a cast in one of her eyes, that made it seem when she was talking to Uncle Hube, as if she was watching me, who only ever offered us cordial. I took it but I never drank it for I was sure that with a name like cordial it would make me drunk.

At another house the couple kept geese that they allowed to roam freely and which, from the outset, made it clear that they did not like strangers, for anyone going near the gate would bring them running and hissing. The first time it happened to me I stood my ground; heroics that were rewarded with blood running from a peck wound on my leg. I didn't bother to hang around after that. As soon as they started coming, I started going.

Despite that I enjoyed delivering to the different houses, especially the one where a dark-haired girl, several months older than me, with whom I became good friends lived. Her name was June, and while her father stood talking to Uncle Hube, June and her mother moved the coal into the coalhouse.

Sometimes she would look over and smile. If her father saw her he would stop his conversation with the instruction "Dunt waste your time starin' at he, get on wi' your work. And you," pointing at me, "Get on round the front of that cart and see to the hoss." Which made me think he was not only a very lazy man, but a most dislikeable one as well.

Sometimes something unplanned happened that could later be seen to be part of an on-going lesson that had to be learned, in order to understand what living in and being a part of the countryside meant, especially in the care and welfare of the animals. It was in such an unplanned way that I received my introduction to the world of the blacksmith's forge and the work that went on there.

It happened one day when we had delivered a load of coal to Westfield and Kit, on the way back, cast one of her shoes on the G.W.R. level crossing at Radstock, causing us to make a visit to Kenny Brimble whose forge was behind the Bell Hotel. He was working on a horse when we arrived, the ring of his hammer on the anvil greeting us as he shaped a shoe from a length of red-hot steel, held firmly in the jaws of a pair of long-handled pliers.

The rhythm of his hammer, the fountains of sparks that flew up with each strike, the smell of horse sweat and steam as each finished shoe was plunged into a trough that held a mixture of water and oil to cool and temper them, all these sights and sounds and smells fascinated me.

Greeting Uncle Hube who explained what had happened, Kenny walked up to Kit, talking to her and patting her neck and withers, before bending to lift up the hoof from which she had cast the shoe and examining it.

"I dunt think she've done herself any damage," he said. "Her foot d'look alright. You'm lucky that happened where it did."

He examined the rest of her shoes and feet then said, "All they shoes could do wi' bein' replaced. They 'ent got a lot of wear left in 'em."

"I d'know," Uncle Hube told him. "I were gwanna come in on Saturday and have'm done. I get'm done now, that'll save I makin' another journey."

We watched as Kenny removed the three remaining shoes and tossed them into a pile in the corner. That was followed by each hoof being examined for cracks or sore spots and any small stones or bits of gravel that may have become lodged in them being removed, before he cut out some of the growth from the centre, called the frog, of the hoof.

Taking a length of flat steel he laid it across the anvil and cut four lengths from it, one of which he put into the fire. Then looking at me for the first time, but speaking to Uncle Hube, he asked, "Who's got there then?"

"Thass my new helper."

"Is 'er any good wi' a shovel?"

"He dunt seem too bad up to now. I can't say how long 'tis gwanna last though."

"Wass reckon about bellows. Think he'd be any good turnin' they?"

"You'll have to ask he that," said Uncle Hube, "I can't answer for'n."

"Wass think then young'un?" Kenny asked, "Reckon you could do that?"

"What's bellows?" I asked him.

He moved across to a narrow drum-shaped fitting on the wall beside the fire that had a handle fixed to it. Taking hold of the handle and telling me to watch the fire, he began turning it slowly. Immediately the fire began to burn hotter.

"This is the bellows," he told me. "What they d'do is pump air into the fire to help it make the metal hot enough to work. But tidn't just a matter of pumping air, it got to be done at the right speed. Not too fast else you'll spoil the metal, and not too slow, else we shall be here all day waitin' for it to get hot enough. You reckon you could do that?"

"I think so," I told him, as I took the handle and began turning it as he had shown me.

His "That's right, keep'n nice and steady," gave me the confidence to relax and enjoy watching him as he placed the lengths of cold steel in the fire, to take them out a while later glowing brightly red and begin hammering them into horseshoes. As each shoe was finished he placed, it while still red-hot, against one of Kit's hooves where, through clouds of acrid smoke, the shape of the shoe was burned into it.

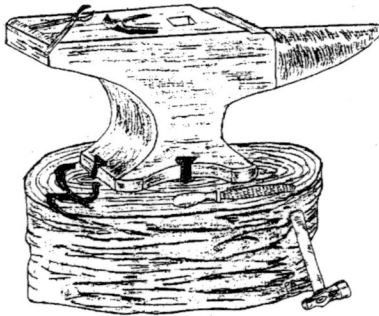

"Does it not hurt her when you put those hot shoes against her feet?" I asked him.

"She dunt feel a thing," he told me. "If that did hurt her, she'd kick I out through the roof. Any road, that baint her feet, that's her toenail. Thass all a horse's hoof is, a big toenail. That dunt cause her any more trouble than gettin' your toenails cut d'cause you."

"Why do you do it?"

"Thass done," he explained, "so that when I d'come to put the shoes on her they d'fit properly. They got to be a good fit, else she'd soon get very sore feet and not be able to walk. 'twould be just like you when you d'get a nail up in your boot."

"Can I come back and turn the bellows for you again?" I asked him when we were leaving.

"I reckon you could," he said, "as long as 'tis alright wi' the gaffer there."

That day was the first of many that I spent at the forge. In addition to turning the bellows, I also sorted the old, different sized, horseshoes into separate piles and swept up the hoof pairings that accumulated when the horses had their hooves cut back and trimmed.

I was not the only one who found pleasure in the forge. On most days, some of the retired miners would gather there to chat and lend a hand with the bellows. In the afternoons on the way home from school and when they were on holiday, many of the children would gather in the doorway and watch as the lengths of steel were turned through cascades of fiery sparks, into horseshoes and other implements.

*   *   *

FOURTEEN

A thing I enjoyed when all my stable jobs were done, was sitting in the shade of the big willow tree that grew in the corner of the stable yard beside the stream and watch the shadows sunbathing in the afternoon glare, while under the tree the dappled sunlight bounced and danced like fireflies across my legs.

One day, when Fred Wallace, I think that's who it was, and I sat watching a blackbird chase its yellow beak across the garden in short bursts of motion, its long tail wagging like an admonishing finger each time it stopped, he suggested that we should follow the stream and find out where it went. Agreeing with him, we took off our boots and stepped into the ankle-deep water.

Immediately behind the privies, the stream entered a low brick-lined tunnel about three feet high. Ducking our heads we began crouching our way slowly toward the pinprick of light that marked the far end. As we sloshed through the water we were accompanied by the squealing and splashing of the rats that inhabited the tunnel. Many of them ran before us in a frenzy of hurried escape while others, rushing their cold wet bodies against our legs and across our feet, dashed past us going the other way.

The tunnel went all the way under our garden and the drummy road, before ending at the foot of the slope on the other side in Mr Craddock's field. As we came out of the tunnel, hens and ducks were running all over the place in terrified confusion as many of the rats left the tunnel and ran toward the railway line.

The stream went on across Mr Craddock's field into another tunnel that took it under the embankment, then across the meadow on the other side until it reached the brook into which it lowered itself gurgling with pleasure.

"If any of they Germans were to come we could use that tunnel to capture them," my companion said, when we were back in the stable yard. "We could creep through and catch 'em easy. They wouldn't expect anyone t'do summat like that."

"And we could take a gun each," I said.

"Dunt be daft. Where be we gwanna get guns from?" he asked.

"Uncle Hube's," I told him. "I'll borrow his twelve-bores. You can have one and I'll have the other."

"He'd go mad if you were to touch his guns. I reckon he'd be a sight wuss than any of they Germans."

"He wouldn't mind if we captured some," I told him. "I reckon he'd be pleased. We might even get a medal."

In the event no Germans came, so the need to borrow the guns never arose. We didn't get a medal either.

What we did get was a more exciting game of Pooh-Sticks. Folding pieces of paper to make sails, we fixed them to our stick boats and put them into the stream by the willow tree then, racing up the garden, we crossed the drummy road and slid down the slope in an effort to reach the other end of the tunnel before the boats emerged.

*　　*　　*

Our return to school brought a temporary halt to my days out on the cart. Though I missed the freedom and travel at first, school was such a happy place I soon accepted that the days were once again more closely governed by the clock.

In school lessons that had been put away in the cupboard of freedom almost two months earlier were brought out again, dusted off and revised. Outside the windows the seasons, each marking their own short life in bright colours, merged at the edges, making it difficult to say where one began and another ended.

Autumn. The time when the trees and hedges put on their most colourful clothes to hide their sadness as another year began drawing to a close. Soon the leaves, silent, sun-filled messengers of summer just past, would travel gently earthward like pieces of shattered rainbows to warm and warn the soil against winter's coming onslaught.

Shedding its dew tears it would wave goodbye to the days of laughter and games in the sunshine, haymaking and harvesting, and signal that soon the potatoes would have to be lifted and mangels and turnips twisted out of the frost-hard ground and stored, much needed food for animals, both human and dumb, through the long, cold days of winter.

Autumn also brought with it the thick damp fogs that filled the valley, sometimes for several days at a time, making the village appear smaller than it did in the sunshine as though the cottages, seeking comfort from each other, had moved to huddle closer together while in the tops of the trees, hidden from view by the fog, birds called out shame to the grey wet drabness that so effectively barred entry to the sun.

As the daylight hours grew shorter and the nights longer and colder, Kit was brought into the stable for the winter. Although it meant that I could no longer ride her up to the field at the end of the day's work, it did mean that I could spend my evenings in the stable with her.

Most times I would bring the piece of tack I was working on out of the tack-room into the stable and sit doing it with my back resting against the manger while Kit watching me, made soothing chomping noises as she ate the hay from the rack above the manger.

When it was time to leave, it was always to the sounds of her snuffling and blowing contentedly on her bed of thick new straw while outside in the yard the cart, its shafts reaching toward the sky, stood as though railing against the coming winter.

The return of early darkness always brought with it the problem of going to the privy, especially if you were of a nervous disposition, for the shadows then gave life to, and a firm belief in, all of the monsters and ghosts we had heard about in the stories we had been told. Those journeys were never made alone if it could possibly be avoided, but always in company with someone.

On the occasions when we had to go by ourselves, the object was to get there and perform the necessary offices as quickly as possible, although they always took longer than we hoped, and back home in record time. Many times, while sitting in a dark cocoon of fear and expectancy, a pair of eyes would suddenly appear over the top of the door and the disembodied voice of their owner would ask, "How's gettin' on then?"

That was the moment when even the most stubborn of bowels were guaranteed to vacate, followed shortly afterwards by the sound of their owners feet kicking chunks of night aside in their desperate rush for home and safety.

*   *   *

The year moved on toward the annual carol service held for the local communities. For several weeks before the service, while descending bombs sang their hymns of hate over the cities and towns of Britain to the tuneless music of air-raid sirens and retaliating guns, we rehearsed well-known carols in the time-honoured 'Peace-on-Earth, Goodwill-to-all-men' manner.

The second school party of the year at Christmas that followed the two or three nights of the carol service, was always held in the school. The screen door between Mrs Symes, who had replaced Miss Chambers, and Mrs Bending's classrooms was folded back to make one large room, which we decorated with school-made paper chains and trimmings. Holly, covered with bright red berries, was brought in from the surrounding area to give the final touch of Christmas to the room.

After the sandwiches, cakes, jellies and trifles had all disappeared, we either played party games or were entertained by a conjuror. The one who came regularly to us, and very good he was too, was Mr Vernon from Bath.

*   *   *

The days between the end of the school term and the day we all waited for with excited anticipation, were spent doing the remaining important tasks. The hen, chosen several days before, was killed and prepared for the oven.

Christmas morning arrived, dark and cold. The clock told us that it was very early to be awake and opening presents, the wrappings of which still seemed to hold the warmth from Santa's hand. The joy, or let-down, when the contents of the packages was known, was felt to varying degrees before sleep claimed us.

Waking later to the smell of fried Christmas pudding, we quickly shivered into our clothes then hurried downstairs to the warm parlour and breakfast. Once the meal was over I set off for the stable where, before starting work, I gave Kit the piece of pudding I had brought for her.

After she was fed, the stable cleaned, and a bed of fresh straw put down, it was up the garden to collect the eggs. The hens would be clustered in a warmth-sharing huddle from which came a low, sad sound, as though they were mourning the loss of the hen we would be eating for dinner later that day.

*   *   *

New Year's day brought no noticeable change to the tenor or tempo of our lives. The days were still firmly held in the bitter grip of Winter's icy hand. Summer gone, now lay at rest behind the shrouding fogs of Autumn, while Summer yet to come, still lay beyond the, as yet, unborn days of Spring.

Resolutions were brought out of storage and renewed with something added to them. Before nightfall, with no conscious assistance on our part, they were returned to Time's cupboard to await the arrival of the next New Year.

Greetings were exchanged, most of them attached to hugs and cuddles, kisses and handshakes, all reinforced with a liquid goodwill. Whatever form they took, they all carried with them the heartfelt hope that it would truly be a 'happy' New Year and before it ended war would be a thing of the past.

*   *   *

Most mornings of Winter would find us waking to a land covered in frost. On such days the air was so clear, distant things appeared to be much closer, sounds were heard with a greater awareness, and our bodies tingled with a freshness that was almost brittle in its nose-nipping, finger-fumbling way.

On the long, cold nights, of Winter, when the outside jobs were finished; when the hens were safely in their houses heated by the warmth of their thickly-feathered bodies; when Kit and Joey were stabled, the hay racks full and deep beds of straw on which to lie; when the buckets had been filled and stood in the scullery to ensure water for both us and them the following morning, should the standpipe outside in the road freeze; on such nights, the most enjoyable thing of all was sitting with mother, my brothers, and Uncle Hube, in front of the fire, watching the flames throw flickering light and shadows onto our faces and into the room behind us, warming us with the heat of sunshine that had struck the earth three hundred million years before.

Sunlight that had given light and warmth to vegetation that now, as coal, burned in a mixture of long ago Autumn's reds, oranges and yellows. Sometimes, in a burst of fitful energy, a pocket of gas within the coal would explode and send up a flame fiercely blue, that died in an instant but which left a lasting impression on mind's eye.

*   *   *

Snowdrops, bowing heads before the regal stateliness of the daffodils and the squat sturdiness of the crocuses, gave the first sign of life returning to the land. Above them in the tall trees, the rooks were again making their noisy return to last year's nests. Lambs appeared in the fields as ewes carried out the final act of a process that had started the previous year.

The hedges and trees were more secretive in the changes they made. It seemed that almost overnight, catkins appeared on the hazel bushes and began waving excited fingers to the sticky buds on the 'conker' trees, while the hedges took on a green haze in a more sedate and refined manner.

However, it was the men pushing wheelbarrows full of gardening tools to the allotments at Braysdown Lane, that told us Spring had really arrived once more.

*   *   *

FIFTEEN

Early **Spring.** Five o' clock in the morning. The beginning of a new day. Carrying two buckets I make my bleary-eyed way out of the house. In the hedges some birds are already awake and beginning to greet the day in a feather-ruffling way.

I stop at the standpipe in the road where, while rubbing the hot tiredness from my eyes, I fill one of the buckets with water, which I carry with me as I continue down to the stable where Kit greets my arrival with welcoming snuffles.

While she drinks from the bucket, I put a measure of oats in the manger and refill the rack above it with hay. Going into the tack-room I carry out the heavy work collar and lean it against the stable wall. The heavy work saddle I place on the floor beside the manger, and the working headstall I hang on a nail by the stable door.

Once those jobs are done I walk back up the road. Birds singing the first of the day's songs make me think of Herksy, who could imitate most of the birds we heard so well it was difficult to tell for sure which was doing the whistling.

I fill the second bucket with water and carry it indoors for use in the house. After washing my hands I sit down and eat my breakfast. Through the open window come the sounds of a slowly awakening day.

Cows lowing softly as they wait to be called in for the first milking; the happy whistling of Chick Gregory, making his milk deliveries; voices calling greetings and wirelesses playing while dogs, lifting legs and barking happily, go off on business of their own. In the tops of the trees rooks, waving wings like black cloaks, call the still sleeping from their beds.

I return to the stable by way of the top garden in order to let the hens out of their houses into the runs, and lift any eggs. At the stable I manage, with Kit's assistance, to get the work collar over her head and sitting correctly on her shoulders. Using an upturned box, I get the work saddle onto her back and the tail stall settled comfortably beneath her tail. The blinkered headstall is less of a problem and takes little time to get the bit in her mouth and the throat-latch buckled. Leading her out of the stable I back her into the cart, put the shafts in their supports and attach the chains to her collar.

91

Leaving her I muck out the stable, leaving the floor to dry while she is out at work; fresh straw will be put down for her when she returns. I lead her out of the yard and up the road to the back door where she waits for Uncle Hube to come out and set off for the pit at Writhlington to begin another day's work.

*   *   *

Spring, continuing its advance on Winter, waved its blossom flags of victory in pink and red and white from the fruit trees, while birds, singing songs of thanks, resumed the job of building a home for soon-to-be-laid eggs. As the days grew milder, Kit and Joey were returned to the field.

One evening we hitched Kit to the cart again and went to the top field to bring back a load of hay for the stable and put some out in the field for Kit and Joey.

Once the cart had been loaded, Uncle Hube cut some to put out in the field. When it was ready George asked if he could carry it up the field to where Joey was standing watching us.

"Better not," replied Uncle, "You know what he's like."

"Please," pleaded George. "He'll be alright when he sees he's being fed."

"Alright then. But you make sure you d'keep your eye on'n."

Digging the fork into the hay, George lifted it up onto his shoulder and set off up the field. He had put the hay on the ground and turned back towards the rick when Joey, true to his nature, decided to forget the hay and eat George instead. With one of his wild kind of screams he took off after George who, seeing his rapid advance, let out an equally wild scream dropped the hay fork and ran.

The fact that the hedge between our field and Joe Gullick's had been just cut and layered, leaving on our side a long row of hedge cuttings waiting to be collected and burned, was what saved George that day. Reaching the row of hedge cuttings he hurdled over them like an olympic steeple-chaser, and tore down the field between them and the hedge to the rick, where he arrived out of breath and very shaken. Joey, meanwhile, had given up the chase and returned to the pile of hay which he was munching on quite contentedly.

That was the last time he was to perform his nasty tricks on either of us for shortly after that incident, much to our pleasure and relief he was sold to a greengrocer at Radstock. April arrived which meant the horse would be grazed in the field at Single Hill, while the top field was left to grow and produce the grass needed to make the winter's hay. The change over always took place on the last Saturday in April and was preceded with one of the jobs I always enjoyed, dung spreading.

One of the pleasures of life is to open up a dung-heap and load the contents on to the cart, then take it to the field and unload it into piles to be spread later.

It required the whole day and most of the dung to cover the entire field, so that by the time we were finished what had been a large heap of manure was reduced to little more than a small mound. It took most of the next day to spread it, but what satisfaction it gave despite tired muscles and an aching back. Just to stand looking at it was enough to convince us it would produce a good crop of hay.

When the grass was ready, Uncle Hube would take a scythe and cut a swath around the tall grass wide enough for the horses pulling the cutter to turn without trampling down the grass at the edges. Not to have done so would have meant the loss of much needed hay.

There is something about the sound a scythe makes as it cuts the standing grass, that is unlike any other sound of the countryside. The 'hushing' of the blade as it lays the tall greenness gently on the ground, is like the sound of a mother whispering to her baby as she places it into the safety of its cot.

Once cut, the grass was left to cure. The length of time it took, generally four or five days, depended largely on how well the weather behaved. During that time, while Uncle Hube carried on with his coal deliveries, George and I would take long-handled hay forks and toss the curing grass, shaking it loose to help with the drying off of any overnight dampness that had gathered, and ensure the sun reached it all.

Once the hay was ready it was raked into long straight rows using either hand rakes or the horse-rake, ready for the horse-drawn sweep to collect it and deliver it to where the new rick was to be built. There, using the hay forks, it was pitched up to the waiting rick builders.

Rick-building day and the men, among whom Cuzz was always one, arrived at the field where they began gently shaking the hay to make sure it was properly dry before they began gathering it in. To build with damp hay could cause heat to build up inside the rick which could result in the hay turning mouldy or, in some cases, catching fire.

One year a land-army girl was among the workers who, instead of getting on with some work like the rest of us, spent her time going round asking questions.

"What's that?" indicating an object.

One of the men would tell her only to be immediately asked, "And what's that?"

"I baint stoppin' here young'un," Cuzz said to me, "She be askin' too many questions for I. I'm gwine on up the top of the field out the way. You comin'?" And picking up a hay rake he walked off. Doing the same, I followed him.

There was to be no escape though, for we hadn't been there for more than a couple of minutes when she came strolling up, and stood watching us for a few minutes before she asked, "What's that?" pointing with her foot to one of the rakes lying on the ground.

"Wass what?" Cuzz looked at me and winked.

"That thing lying there."

"What thing lying where?"

"That," she snapped, stretching her leg and bringing her foot down on the upturned teeth of the rake, causing the long handle to shoot up and catch her a very hard smack across her large, green-jumpered chest, making her exclaim loudly in a pain-filled voice, "Oh, bother the rake."

"Thass what 'tis right enough," said Cuzz, as she turned away rubbing her chest. "That be a rake. I reckon you'll know what 'tis next time you d'see one."

"I'll bet she felt that," I said, as we watched her walk away down the field.

"I 'spect she did," he agreed. "You should have offered to rub it for her. That would have made thee both feel better.

*   *   *

There were three breaks during the day, at mid-morning, at midday, and one in the afternoon. During the first break, while the horse enjoyed a rest and drink of water and the men a mug of tea, two of us carried the cider jar to the Apple Tree where Mrs Drew filled it. We shared the job of carrying the filled jar back to the field, where we would safely leave it in the shade until it was required.

The longest break was at midday, when we all sat down in the shade of the rick and ate our sandwiches, the men washing theirs down with mugs full of the amber liquid from the cider jar. Watching them drink it with such obvious relish, made us wonder what it tasted like.

When we asked we were told not to go worrying our heads about things like that. An answer that meant the only way we were going to find out was to taste it for ourselves. The following day on the way back from the Apple Tree, Lennie and I did just that.

Stopping out of the sight of the houses when we reached the cinder path, we twisted the cork out of the jar and each took a nervous sip. Lennie spat his out but I thought it was nice. So nice, that I took several more swallows before replacing the cork and continuing our journey back to the field where, out of sight of the resting men, I took another long drink before putting the jar down under the rick in the shade and sitting down beside them.

The next thing I knew was being shaken by Ern Gulliver. Sitting up, I found myself looking into the grinning faces of the men.

"You d'seem a bit tired today," Ern said. "What time did you get to bed last night?"

"My usual time," I told him.

"Well you couldn't have slept very well, else you'd be able to do your work."

"I have been doing my work," I said, wondering what he was going on about. "I didn't stop 'til everyone else did, then I went with Lennie to get the cider."

"We d'know all that," said Edgar Swift, "But you didn't start back wi' the rest of us did thee? And from what I can see it dunt look as if you'm gwanna do a lot more today."

"Course I am," I told him. "When the breaks over."

"Wass mean, when the breaks over? He's over and done wi'. You'd know that if you didn' spend all your time sleepin'"

The rest of that day was the worst time I had ever known. I was continually being sick, my legs and arms felt like lead and my head, an ecstasy of pain, throbbed so much that I just wanted to lie down and never move again.

Seeing the misery of my suffering and being my friend, Cuzz gave me no comfort at all. He just kept saying that I would work it out of me if I kept going. I didn't like him very much that afternoon. To be honest, I didn't like him at all.

Finally the rick was built, and all that remained were the small amounts of hay that had fallen off the sweep as each load was taken in. They would be raked up the following day. As soon as Uncle Hube gave the word, I set off with Kit to the stable where while I unharnessed her and rubbed her down, the rumblings of pleasure she gave sounded like thunder to my pounding head.

I had almost finished when Uncle Hube walked into the stable and with a hard slap knocked me off my feet and dumped me on my backside on the floor. Head swimming, I sat there looking up at him through pain and tear-filled eyes.

"That's what you d'get for drinkin' that stuff," he said. "You ever do that again and you'll really know all about it."

Getting slowly to my feet I stood looking at him.

"How did you know?" I asked him. "Who told you."

"Who told me? No-one told me. No-one needed to tell me. I knew what you'd been up to even before I saw they hayseeds in the cider."

With that he walked into the tackroom, leaving me to finish Kit and take her to the field down Single Hill.

Something I always did at the end of the day was ride from the stable to the field. That day as I was about to get my aching body on to Kit's back, he came back out of the tackroom and stopped me.

"I dunt want to see thee up on her back," he said. "She've done a days work while you bin lyin' about sleepin'. You just walk her down there nice and slow."

*   *   *

When the remaining hay was raked up and put on the rick, it was left to settle while we took the cart to one of the farms to collect the straw for thatching. Back at the field, the straw was off-loaded beside the rick where, each of us taking a bundle, we 'combed' it out with our fingers to make sure that the stalks were straight and lying correctly before the thatching began.

Once settled the rick was pulled, which meant removing all the loose hay from around the sides. This not only tidied them up and saved valuable hay, it also made them waterproof against the rain and snow that would beat against them.

Thatching, another job I enjoyed, required a high level of experience and skill to do it properly. Like most things, I was told, starting at the bottom of the ladder was the only way to learn how to do any job correctly, and that is where I began; on the ground passing up the bundles of straw as they were needed. When I was finally allowed up onto the rick, it was with the admonition to 'make sure you d'face the open end of the straw downwards, else the weather'll get in and ruin the hay.'

Each year an oldish man named Parsons came to help with the thatching, although the speed he went up and down the ladder belied his age. One day when we thought he would be attending a funeral, he turned up ready for work.

"Wass thou doin' here then?" Uncle Hube asked him. "I thought you were gwine to a funeral."

"I dunt go to funerals," was the reply. "I dunt mind goin' to weddin's and chris'nin's, but not funerals."

We worked in silence putting the bundles of straw beside the ladder ready for thatching before Uncle Hube said, " Wass mean, you dunt go to funerals?"

"What I d'say. I dunt go to funerals."

Another silence then, "Well that's as maybe, but I'll tell thee there's one funeral you wunt be able to miss."

"Oh, ah! An' which one's he then?"

"Your own. You'm gwanna have to go to that'n."

"Well I reckon you could be wrong there as well, cos I wunt be goin' to he either, not unless somebody d'come and take I. But that wunt happen for a long time yet. Our family d'live for years once they bin born. You take my gran'father. He were most ninety when he went, and even then he didn' die. He went and fell off a cart he were drivin' and got hisself killed."

Once the work of haymaking and thatching was done, we helped gather the grain harvest growing in other fields. We didn't enjoy the harvesting as much as the haymaking, for the sheaves were rough where the stalks had broken and our arms were soon all scratched and sore. Also the stubble left by the cutter was stiff and dug into our ankles, making them as sore as our arms.

At break-times, it was difficult to find a place where it was comfortable to sit while we ate our sandwiches. Even though we sat on our rolled-up shirts and jackets, the hard stubble still managed to poke us through them.

Walking behind the horse-drawn binder, we watched the sails push the cut corn on to the belt which delivered it to the rear of the machine where it was tied into sheaves and then, by means of several long steel tines, thrown out on to the ground. Our job was to stand the sheaves upright in stooks in such a way as to allow any breeze to pass through them and assist with the drying, but which would not blow over in a sudden gust.

As the corn was cut, any animals hidden in it kept moving inward away from the binder until, with all cover gone, they were forced to bolt. Then the guns and dogs brought along for that purpose would come into use. Nothing to beat a plate of rabbit stew after a hard day in the field.

Once the stooks were dry they were built into ricks and either thatched or covered with a large canvas sheet. The threshing machines would come later to finish the job.

As each field was finished we would glean it for any ears of corn left by the binder. This gave us a lot of free grain which we fed to Kit and the hens.

While the top field was recovering Kit remained down Single Hill. One evening Brian Warren came to the door to tell us that she had got down into the brook and couldn't get out. We found her standing in the water, exhausted by her efforts to rescue herself.

"You'm gwanna have to get up on her back and ride her out," Uncle Hube said, which was easy enough to say but rather more difficult to achieve, but by climbing one of the trees and going out along a branch, I managed to lower myself on to her back. It was then a simple matter to ride her down to the bridge and up the low bank into the field.

Later that evening when we went back to check on her, we found she was still not recovered from her ordeal.

"I reckon," said Uncle Hube, as he stood rubbing her head, "'tis time I got myself another hoss and sent you away into retirement."

I looked at him open-mouthed for I couldn't believe what he was saying. When Joey had gone both George and I were happy, but Kit? To talk of sending her to a place I had never even heard of made the tears spring to my eyes. Didn't he realise how much we loved her?

"Will we be able to go and see her?" I asked him.

"Go where and see her?" he wanted to know.

"That place Retirement you're going to send her to."

"You girt gowk," he said laughing. "That baint a place. Thass what d'happen when you'm too old to work any more. She wunt be gettin' sent away. She'll bide here in the field and have a long holiday.

Shortly afterwards Prince, a big chestnut horse arrived. To describe him as anti-social understates the true nastiness of his nature. Kicking and biting were his main sources of enjoyment, while for relaxation he liked nothing better than to lean his great weight against you while you were mucking out, squashing you between himself and the stable wall.

Harnessing him was an exercise that required both speed and anticipation, in order not to be where large unfriendly teeth snapped together, and hooves caused miniature gales as they swept past.

As Ern Gulliver said, "If thik hoss were a dog you'd have'n put down."

His attitude, as far as Uncle Hube was concerned, was no reason not to have him ready for work on time. "If he d'kick thee, then kick'n back. If he d'bite thee, then bite'n back," was all he said when we tried to explain the difficulties we were having.

When the grass in the top field had recovered he was grazed there, leaving the quiet peace of the field at Single Hill to Kit and her sadly, very short retirement. We found her dead there one morning in October.

*   *   *

SIXTEEN

The **last big outside job** of the year was the checking and repairing of the fences around the top field. We had finished the top fence between us and the rec and the fence separating us from Jack Craddock's field, and had just started digging a post hole for the bottom fence beside the cinder path, when a woman and two grown-up girls came walking along.

They stopped beside us and while they stood watching, the two girls kept nudging one another and giggling like a pair of dafties, until we had finished the post-hole we were digging. Then the woman, trying to make her voice sound posh said, "That looks like hard work."

"Dunt do thee any harm," answered Uncle Hube.

"What doesn't?" asked the woman.

"Hard work."

"Are you going to bury something?" she asked, to the obvious amusement of the two girls.

"Only me troubles," he told her.

"Have you done that sort of work all your life?" she wanted to know.

"Not yet," was his reply.

The next question that was asked by one of the girls, had me staring at her in amazement. Stepping closer to me she pointed at Prince and asked, "Why hasn't that cow got any horns?"

I was about to answer when Uncle Hube, putting his hand on my shoulder and squeezing it gently, stopped me. Then resting his arms on one of the posts he stood for a while looking up across the field before he spoke.

"Well," he said finally, not taking his eyes off the field, "There be a lot o' reasons why cows dunt have horns. Some be born wi'out them, some d'lose them fightin' or d'knock'm off agin the wall. Others d'get horns what d'grow twisted and the vet d'cut they off, else they'd grow into their eyes and blind'm. But the main reason thik cow there got no horns is because he's a hoss."

The silence that followed was almost deafening, but it did put an end to any further questions. Saying not another word they took themselves off along the cinder path. I did notice as they left, that the girls had stopped their stupid giggling.

*   *   *

Another incident involving Prince took place the following year, soon after he had been returned to the field at Single Hill. As he was such a bad-tempered and unpredictable animal we put a 'Beware of the Horse' sign on the gate, which one of the local boys, showing an unexpected bent for comedy changed to 'Beware of the Grasshopper'.

The following day at school, hearing him bragging about it, I bet him he wouldn't go into the field, walk up to Prince, and feed him an apple. Being a hero, he took me up on it.

When school was finished we made our way to the field where Prince was standing under some tall elder bushes at the top of the field beside the cottages. After carefully sizing up the situation, the budding comedian climbed over the gate and began walking up the field toward him.

Although he had never shown the slightest tendency toward a sense of humour Prince, deep down, must have enjoyed a bit of fun. With raised head he watched until the boy got well into the field before, with his ears flat to his head and teeth bared in a big smile of welcome, and looking nothing at all like any grasshopper I had ever seen, he came pounding toward him to say hullo.

His totally unexpected greeting caused the boy to quickly rearrange his plans so, instead of waiting to feed him, he decided to give him a race. Not being fast enough to reach the gate he did the only thing he could and that was to jump in the brook, where he waded across to the other side and set off home.

Prince, meanwhile, continued his gallop down to the gate causing me to step back out of his reach. Waiting until his ears were pricked again, I fed him the apple I had brought. I always had something for him as a kind of insurance policy against kicks and bites, but which never had any affect on his behaviour.

Leaving him I set off up the hill. As I walked past the station gate, the boy's mother came rushing up and grabbing me began shaking me furiously, demanding to know why I had let a dangerous horse loose on her son.

I tried to explain but right then she was in no mood to listen to any explanations. All I got was several very hard slaps around the head and ears.

My ears were still sore the next morning but I didn't mind. I knew his were going to be a lot more sore when I saw him. Not because his mother had warmed mine, but because his lies had caused her to do so.

For a long time afterwards I called him 'grasshopper'. I know he didn't like it, but he got used to it.

*　　*　　*

Threshing-time arrived and groups of men gathered beside the grain stacks, beside which stood the large threshing machine. Once the thatch or tarpaulin had been removed, wire netting was put around the stacks and several of the men climbed on to them and began pitching the sheaves to the men on the thresher.

They fed the sheaves into the drum where the grain was threshed out into shoots at the ends of which hung the empty sacks waiting to be filled. As each sack became full, a lever was pushed across which diverted the grain into another empty sack while the filled one was unhooked and tied and replaced with another empty one. The straw was flung out on to the ground and loaded on to carts to be used as winter bedding for the livestock and for the following year's thatching.

As the stacks grew smaller, the rats that infested them were forced to move down until they had nowhere left to go. That was when the dogs were put inside the netting. The barks and growls, squeaks and squeals, of battle, went on until all the rats had been destroyed. Their carcasses were later loaded into sacks and carried away for disposal.

It wasn't only at threshing time that rats featured in our lives. Many times from our bedroom window, we watched as they came out from beneath the pigeon loft and ranged about the garden, only to disappear at the slightest hint of danger. They didn't always escape, for many times the cat or a well-placed shot reduced their numbers. Once, when I was cleaning out the rabbit's hutch, I heard Uncle Hube come up and stand behind me.

"That's a big'un," he said quietly.

"What is?" I asked him.

"That rat up there in the flight. Down in the corner by the loft," he answered.

Looking to where he indicated I saw it, well almost saw it, for only the front part of its face was showing.

"I can just see it," I told him.

"Right," he said, "I d'want you to stand still and keep your eye on'n. I dunt want thee to move or turn round no matter what you d'hear behind thee. I'm gwanna pop back in the house for a minute."

I heard him leave and return shortly and stand behind me again, then out of the corner of my eye I saw the barrels of his twelve-bore slowly poke forward over my shoulder.

"Duck down slowly," he told me, "and cover your ears."

I'd hardly started to move when the gun went off deafening me so much I didn't hear the empty cartridge case hit the flag-stones beside me.He got the rat though. Blew it right out of the hole.

*   *   *

In most communities there is always someone who is regarded as a character. Such a person was Joe Sharland who lived at Shoscombe Bottom. One day Frank and Butch were sitting on the hump at the foot of Greenstreet, all that was left, so we had been told, of the house in which the words of the National Anthem had been written, when Joe came along and sat down beside them.

"I'm glad you'm here," he said, "I got summat to tell thee."

"Wass that then?" they asked him.

"What happened to I 'tother night."

"What were that?"

"That bloke what were followin' I."

"Followin' thee where?" Frank asked.

"Well I were on me way back home and were comin' through Ruckley Ford, when I heard these footsteps comin' on behind I so I stopped and wass think, they stopped as well. Then when I started up again they started up again. If I did speed up, darned if they didn't speed up. Well now I thought to meself, Joe I thought, you'm gwanna trick whoever that is. So I pulled the collar of me jacket up round me ears so that whoever 'twer wouldn't be able to see the white of me shirt, and ducked in behind one o' they trees. And wass thou think? He walked right past and never saw I. And that's who 'twer."

"Wass mean, thass who 'twer?" they wanted to know. "Who were it?"

"I dunt know," he told them, "'twer too dark to see."

He also had a fund of stories. One of them involved his mother who claimed the house was haunted because she heard voices and loud thumps at night. She made these claims for a long time, despite the doubts of the people she told, including the vicar.

She proved in the end she was not hallucinating when it was discovered that due to a fault in the rock, she had been able to hear the voices of the miners underground at Foxcote. The loud thumps had been caused by blasting as the men drove the roads needed to get the coal.

He lived with his sister who he told us, walked in her sleep. "Every night she d'rise from her bed, clean the house and set the table ready. Then when I d'get up to go to work, she d'always get up wi' I to make me breakfast, and ev'ry mornin' she d'say the same thing.

"You shouldn' keep gettin' up during the night to help I," she d'tell I. "I can do my work when you'm gone to the pit."

"I d'tell her tidn't I what d'do it, tis you yourself." but she dunt believe I cos she can't remember doin' it."

Another 'bit of a character' was a man named Moon, known to everyone as 'Shilling'. One night a group of us were outside the Seven Stars pub in Timsbury when Shilling came cycling along the road. As he cycled past the constable called out to him, "Shilling, you've got no lights on that bike."

"You'm right there," came Shillin's reply, as he cycled on into the darkness, "An' you got no bike."

*   *   *

The year passed on its way and Autumn, yawning its tired way out of hibernation, strode across the land painting the leaves and turning the landscape once again into a bedlam of colours, signalling to Summer that its time of residence with us was again nearing its end.

With its return came the fogs, heavy dews and the early darkness of shortening days. Once more the horse was brought into the stable to await the return of better weather. The only time he saw the top field was when we took the cart to fetch a load of hay back to the stable for him

Early on one of those mornings, when it was not yet light but still not dark, with the wind blustering its way through the trees causing them to flail their branches as though they were fighting off meddlesome insects, I saw a ghost. We were in the stable when Uncle Hube found the whetstone he used to sharpen blades, had been left in the field under the rick. As he needed it then, he sent me to fetch it.

Leaving the stable I started up the hill and had reached the corner above Dyson's house, when a white shape that came out of the hedge and floated across the road to the other bank, brought me to a sudden, mouth-drying stop. I knew that I had to get the stone, but how? There was no way I was going to be grabbed by any ghost, for that's what it was, while trying to get past it.

It was the ghost itself that gave me the answer. As it began moving again so did I. Turning, I legged it back down the hill to the stable.

"You were quick," said Uncle Hube, as I fell through the doorway. "But you

didn't need to run all the way there and back. You could have taken your time."
Then holding out his hand, "Let's have'n then."

"I haven't got it," I told him.

"Wass mean thou hassent got it? I told thee exactly where I put'n. I dunt reckon you tried very hard to find'n or you would've. You just get yourself back up there and dunt come back wi'out it."

The only other way was up across Siletons which we had been forbidden to use as the steep slope was too dangerous on dark icy mornings, but going back up the hill was definitely out. Knowing I would be in real trouble if I was seen, Siletons was still the better of the two choices I had, so that was the one I took. I found the whetstone where I had been told it would be and hurried back to the stable by the same route.

While he was sharpening the blade of the chaff cutter, he explained why he had sent me back to the field. "See young'un, 'tis all a question of bein' reliable. I got to know that I can rely on thee when I d'give thee a job t'do. I dunt have the time to worry about whether 'tis bein' done or not I got t'know 'tis, even though I baint there."

I thought that was an end to it until that evening when we were back in the stable cutting chaff, and Mr Gray came in to see Uncle Hube. When they had finished talking he turned to me.

"What happened to you this mornin' then?" he asked, "I heard thee comin' up behind so I waited for thee. Next thing I knew you were dappin' back down the hill wi' sparks comin' out the soles of your boots."

I didn't know what to say, so I said nothing.

"When I heard thee goin' back down the hill I thought you'd zid a ghost or somethin'. You hadn' though, had thee? Mind, that sheet of newspaper what were flappin' about up at the corner could've made a person think they were zein' a ghost. Had I thinkin' for a bit when I saw it movin' about. I reckon if it had moved again, I'd of trotted off home as well."

"Oh ah!" said Uncle Hube, "That's why I thought you'd bin a bit smartish gettin'up that field and back. You let a bit of paper frighten thee cos you thought 'twer a ghost."

*   *   *

Ice-cold mornings and freezing linoleum, so cold against our feet that it felt as though they were burning, told us in the clearest way that Winter had returned. Every morning we would hurry downstairs to the scullery and wash, before sitting down at the table in front of the thawing warmth of the fire. Breakfast over, it was out to do our jobs before setting off for school.

Mother, with comfort in mind, bought several flour sacks which, after she had removed the stitching from the bottom and cut along one of the sides, she boiled to make backings for rag rugs.

Any articles of clothing that could no longer be worn were washed and dried and cut into pieces about an inch wide and three inches long, then using carpet needles we pulled each piece through the sacking until we had warm rugs for all the bedrooms. They certainly made getting out of bed on those cold mornings so much easier.

*   *   *

SEVENTEEN

Another New Year arrived and began its journey to meet the coming Spring, my favourite time of the year. Freezing cold gave way to cold which in turn gave way to mild and the birds began again the annual job of nest-building, egg laying and young rearing. Buds became leaves and night's darkness began its work a little later each day. As soon as the frosts were over, Prince was again left out in the field overnight, which meant that he had to be collected every morning and brought back to the stable, a task that could take up to an hour.

One morning on the way to get him, I passed Mr Gill coming along the cinder path. I was about to climb through the fence into the field when he stopped and called me back to him.

"I've got a job for you and your brother if you d'want it," he said.

"What kind of job?" I wanted to know.

"Deliverin' the eve'nin' papers. You'd have to go down the station and collect 'em off the train from Bath. There's only about fifty a night durin' the week. On Saturday there's more cos some on'm d'take the pink sports paper as well. The pay's six shillings a week."

"I'll have to ask mother first and see what she says," I told him.

"Right," he said, "you ask her and let I know."

With the warning "That it wont mean you can get out of doing your other jobs, you'll have to fit the paper round in with them," mother agreed. It didn't take much to fit it in, especially as the six shillings was almost doubled by the tips we received from the people.

*　　*　　*

Each evening coming up from the station, I would stop for a while beside Jim Swansbury's garden to play with a brown and white pup they had. One evening Jim's father came out of the house walked across to the garden fence.

"You d'like thik pup dunt thee Pad?" he said.

"Yes I do," I told him, "I think he's smashing."

"I reckon he d'like thee as well cos he's always pleased to see thee. I'll bet you'd like to take'n on home with thee."

106

"I would, but I can't do that. He's yours."

"I d'know he's mine, but I already got a dog and I reckon thik pup would be happy livin' wi' you, so he's yours if you d'want'n."

"To keep for always?"

"Course. I'm givin' him to thee."

He picked the pup up and handed him to me. Unable to hide my pleasure, I took him and put him in the bag with the papers, gave Jim's dad the best thank you I could, and went off to deliver the papers.

Rustler I named him after a dog on a wireless programme called Riders of the Range, and we went everywhere together. From the outset he made it clear he was a most independent animal who would generally, but not always, do as he was told for a lot depended on the mood he was in. If anyone tried to impose their will on him they would be rewarded with rumbling growls from deep in his throat. On the other hand, he was capable of the most unexpected loyalty, as he showed clearly one morning when he went with me to collect the accumulator.

As usual the 'tin chapel' gang were waiting. However, that morning things took a completely unexpected turn for as one of them grabbed at me Rustler, snarling and growling, went for him ripping the sleeve of his jacket. Having only their safety and well-being in mind, they all promptly leapt up on to the high wall that ran alongside the road and sat there out of harm's way while Rustler, still showing his displeasure, made several unsuccessful attempts to jump up beside them.

I don't who was the most surprised, them or me, as we all kept looking at him not knowing what to do or say.

"He's mad," the boy who's sleeve he'd ripped said. "He nearly had I."

"Only because you came for me," I told him, "He didn't seem to think much of that. Now he knows you wont do it again you can come down off the wall."

"We'm not comin' down afore he's gone. Look at'n. He's just waitin' for us to come down so that he can get his teeth into one on us."

"You'm not frightened of him are you? Look at'n. He's only a little'un."

"We dunt care what size he is. He's still mad. He were gwanna bite I. Look at what he've done to my sleeve. No, we'm bidin' here 'til he's gone."

That was the last time I ever had trouble with that group, especially if I had Rustler with me. Needless to say I always made sure he was.

Another mystery was the effect he had on Prince. Until then catching him had been a battle every morning, for getting him to stand still long enough to get the halter on him was a day's work in itself. Rustler's presence seemed to quieten him down for instead of charging all over the field when I went to fetch him, as soon as he heard Rustler bark he came across to the fence and stood as quietly as Kit had done while I put the halter on him.

Harnessing him and getting him hitched to the cart was also done more quickly, although he still exercised his teeth and hooves. On mornings when he decided to play up, a growl from Rustler was all it took to make him behave.

*　　*　　*

While several battles in my own personal war appeared to be over, there was still much to keep us aware of the bigger war still being fought across the world. Although the planes that throbbed overhead during the night had become so much a part of our lives that we heard them only as background noises, and though much of the nervous anticipation we felt when the distinctive sound of enemy bombers was heard had left us, we still sat quietly with the wireless turned down until the comfort of friendly silence returned.

As they flew the planes released strips of foil to disrupt the signals picked up by the radar screens. The morning after a bombing raid, we would go out and collect large amounts of the foil which we called 'radio location'.

*　　*　　*

The news that there was a prisoner-of-war in the village, set us asking questions that Uncle Hube called the 'wonders'. "Wonder who he is?" "Wonder what he's like?" "Wonder where he comes from?" "Wonder where they caught him?" "Wonder if he still has his gun?"

He turned out to be a friendly young Italian with black hair, brown eyes, a nice smile, but no gun. There was nothing different or dangerous about him and the warning that we were to stay away from him, was all the invitation we needed to get to know him. Many times we sat on the stile at the bottom of Sileton's where while we did our best to teach him English he tried, without success, to teach us Italian.

As a prisoner-of-war he was not allowed into any of the shops. Undercover job number one was to go to Filer's and buy him cigarettes. Undercover job number two was to help him smoke them. I gave up after a few puffs. It made me feel sicker than the cider had done. I don't remember how long he stayed in the area, but I do recall we were rather put out when we heard he had been taken away. He was really nice.

He wasn't the only person who was made a prisoner in the village for one night during the winter we captured one of our own, and almost repeated the act several weeks later with another that turned out to be a case of mistaken identity.

The successful capture came about when one of the local boys became a victim of his own stupidity. He had graduated from the game we called 'tip and

108

run', to what he considered was the more exciting game of 'hurling the stone'. This was played by creeping up to the door of the house he had chosen and launching a large stone at it with as much force as he could. For some reason he had decided to make our door his number one target.

Several times the house shook as the stone smashed against the door, setting our hearts pumping and the dogs barking and growling. His big mistake was not taking Uncle Hube into consideration, the silly, silly, boy, for one night, instead of being in the house, Uncle Hube was outside waiting for him.

Suddenly the door flew open and in came Uncle Hube with the boy who, feet clear of the ground, struggled to break free of the grip of the big hand firmly attached to his neck. Across the parlour to the lower cellar he carried him and dumped him inside. There in the blackness he stayed for the rest of the evening with only the scurrying mice and his tears for company.

When he was finally released it was with the warning to "Bide along your own bit from now on. I catch thee along here again, I shall pop my hand off your backside." At least he had the gumption not to target our door again.

*   *   *

Saturday afternoons. Queuing at the bottom of the stone steps outside the Palace cinema in Radstock. One of a crowd of happy, noisy, children, waiting to enter the world of Gene Autry, Roy Rogers, Hoppalong Cassidy, Flash Gordon, Tarzan, and many others that lay hidden behind its doors. Heroes and villains brought to life in the flickering light of 'Artful' Chivers's projector.

We knew nothing then of the children and parents who, in other countries, also queued to pass through doors, not into the happy, make-believe world of the pictures, but into the world of eternity, courtesy of cyanide tablets and hate.

The Wallace family as well as being nice neighbours were also good friends to us. Doug and Frank were especially kind and often offered to take George and me with them when they went to the pictures on Monday evenings. Most times mother made us refuse, though there were occasions when she did let us go. It was while we were on our way home on one of those evenings that we almost captured what we thought was a spy.

We had reached the path at the foot of Little Wood near the bottom of Gaston's hill, when the sight of a man squeezing through the wire fence beside the railway line stilled our chatter and brought us to a halt. It was the torch he carried that told us immediately what he was as he walked along the track toward the stile at the far end.

"I'll bet thee anything he's one of they Five Colonists the policeman told us about at school," someone whispered.

"'tis Fifth Columnists, not Five Colonists," Doug corrected him. "But I reckon you could be right even though he 'an't got a bike. Let's follow'n and see what he's up to."

Trailing a suspicious person isn't as easy as it sounds, especially when it's dark, for the night-time world is not at all the same place you know in daylight. Humps and hollows seem to become higher and deeper; trees and bushes appear to have moved while at the same time, leaving their roots lying in an ideal position to trip the careless and unwary, and gates and holes in hedges seem not to be where you always thought they were. There were times when it seemed they had disappeared altogether.

From a distance we watched him climb over the stile and then, nothing. He seemed to simply disappear, making us stop in nervous anticipation, waiting. The darkness ahead remained still and undisturbed so we moved on again until we came to the stile and climbed over it. As we passed the bridge over the railway leading down to Holdway's farm, we saw him again, crouched in the shadow of the parapet.

We carried on until we reached the foot of Greenstreet, where we gathered around Doug to plan the best way to handle the situation.

"We got t'do somethin' about'n," said Doug. "We got to capture'n if we can. If we d'let'n get away, he'll tell they planes where to drop their bombs."

Someone else, no doubt with the Victoria Cross in mind, suggested that we should ambush him and take him to Red Post police station. Good idea. We knew all about ambushes. We saw them most Saturdays at the pictures.

So we lay in hiding as the man walked down the track on a journey that, even if he wasn't shot, was leading him into long years in captivity. We watched him come through the gate and walk on along the road, while we waited for the signal that for some reason never came.

We found out later that the man had been visiting relations at Writhlington, and had been on his way back to Single Hill to catch the train back into Bath. He had not been hiding from us when we had seen him crouched down on the bridge, he had been answering a call of nature. Dirty devil. He should have done it in the woods the same as we did.

Throughout that Winter and the following Spring, the trains that passed were much longer. Some carried mysterious objects with strange shapes hidden beneath green canvas covers. Those carrying service people had more coaches filled to bursting. The only real difference as far as we were concerned, was the added pleasure they gave us by taking longer to pass.

*   *   *

June 6th 1944. On a bright sunny morning we were brought rushing from our houses by the sound of planes that was like nothing we had ever heard before.

The sight that met our upturned faces was the most exciting we had ever seen. The sky was filled with large bombers, each one towing a glider. On and on they went and as each wave disappeared from view, another wave appeared over the houses. Hour after hour they came and went with ear numbing noise.

As we watched one of the towing wires separated and the glider began losing height. Round it flew getting lower and lower until it was forced to land in a field at Foxcote. In the following few minutes most of the surrounding area became almost deserted as nearly every child, along with many of the grown-ups, streamed up across the fields to see it.

We arrived to find half a dozen of the local men armed with shotguns already there and who, following the orders of a police sergeant, kept us well back. If there had been anyone in the glider they must have left before we got there, for we saw no sign of anyone getting out.

Standing about looking at something you can't get near, becomes boring after a while and a diversion is needed. That day a wasps nest in the bank, some carbide Ilfey had brought with him, and an empty lemonade bottle, provided it.

First we hacked a big lump of earth out of the bank then, as there was no tap water available we filled the bottle with the next best thing into which Ilfey poured the carbide. We screwed the top on as tightly as we could and pushed it, while trying not to get stung, well into the hole where the wasps nest was, and sealed the opening with the lump of earth before standing well back in a 'light the blue touchpaper and retire' sort of exercise.

From a safe distance we waited. Ilfey must have been over generous with his carbide for the blast when it came was so strong, it blew a hole in the bank deep enough to swim in had it been filled with water. It certainly sent everyone there diving for cover. The result, of course, was that we got the rough edge of everyone's tongue once they realised it wasn't the beginning of a German invasion. Grown-ups have no sense of humour.

*　　*　　*

There are times in our lives when the actions of others tap hidden depths within us that we had no idea we possessed, and bring out unexpected qualities. It was the parachutists in their gliders and the D-Day landings that brought into being two of the best kept secrets of the war. The Braysdown Parachute Regiment and the Braysdown and Woodborough Combined Commando Unit.

Although the parachute regiment had only two members, Bern and Frank Weston, the damage they could have inflicted on the enemy was limitless. Their training ground was one of the two tall trees at the foot of Sileton's. Their parachute was one of Mrs Weston's large umbrellas.

Climbing the tree, they inched their way along one of the thick branches where, sitting side by side and holding tightly to the handle of the umbrella, they launched themselves into the space beneath their feet.

Bern landed first, spreading his body across the ground in such a way as to allow Frank a fairly soft landing. Once they had recovered their breath, Bern looked at Frank and asked, "Wass land on top of I for? That were bloomin' sore."

"Cos you'm supposed to roll out the way like they do in the pictures," Frank told him, "And you didn't."

The commando unit consisted of three members, Bern, Frank and 'Codger' Young, who had a dinghy. Their training ground was the pond at Woodborough where they put the dinghy in the water and began rowing out to the centre of the pond where a hollow iron post stood several feet above the surface. Having reached it Codger, despite warnings from the other two, decided to climb onto it and scan the surrounding area. As he did so one of the enemy, disguised as a large male swan, came swimming quickly toward them.

Realising the danger Bern and Frank dipped the oars and began rowing, leaving him sitting on top of the post. They had almost reached the safety of the bank when Codger, seeing the danger of the situation, gave a loud Tarzan-like yell, dived into the water and began churning it to a froth as he swam after them.

* * *

A week after D-Day, Germany launched the first of their new type of weapon against us. Nicknamed either 'doodlebugs' or 'buzz bombs', they were pilotless flying weapons guided to their intended targets by gyro compass.

No sooner had the population become used to those flying 'bombs', than they had to face a new and even more destructive weapon in the shape of the V2 rockets. The first fell on England in September, but despite the fear and destruction they brought the lights went on again in parts of London for the first time in more than five years.

In August, during our summer holiday, Dad, who was in the Merchant Navy, came home on leave for only the second time during the war. His ship had been torpedoed and the survivors had been sent on two weeks leave, most of which I remember he spent sleeping.

War news continued to occupy most of us through the end of nineteen forty-four and the beginning of nineteen forty-five. American forces, the wireless informed us, had retaken one place, while the Russians had taken another. The R.A.F. were continuing to bomb targets in Germany, and our soldiers had advanced another thirty miles during the last three days.

On the twelfth of April President Roosevelt died and on the twenty-fourth Berlin was surrounded. Mussolini, the Italian leader, was executed by partisans on the twenty-eighth. On the thirtieth Hitler committed suicide to escape punishment for the holocaust he had inflicted upon the world.

The most important news came on May the eighth. Victory in Europe, V.E. Day. After almost six years of fighting the war was over and street parties were held in celebration. On May the tenth our sister Myra was born.

August 6th 1945. America dropped the first atomic bomb on Hiroshima, bringing about Japan's surrender. Although the next day was named V.J. Day, the formal surrender did not take place until the second of September.

*   *   *

EIGHTEEN

The end of hostilities in Europe brought to many of the evacuees the excitement of preparing for their return to the towns and cities they had lived in before the war. How much a part of them the village and the people had become over the years they only realised on their last day at school, when the pain of parting brought tears to many of them One girl, Joan Marsh, hugging Mrs Bending, asked through her tears if their was some way she could be allowed to stay.

Other families in addition to ours, who for a variety of reasons either couldn't or had no desire to go back, remained in the village. Mrs Collins, Sylv's mum, who made the nicest bread pudding I had ever tasted, stayed with her family, as did Mrs Nicholls and Johnny.

The year, bringing with it a fuller understanding of the damage the war had done and the cost of rebuilding not only the infrastructure, but also trust among the peoples of many countries, passed on its way. Nature, showing her anger at man's folly, produced a grain harvest of such low quality that a world shortage of wheat resulted, causing bread to be rationed for the first time.

At the same time the cost of cigarettes rose from 2/4d to 3/4p for a packet of twenty, although what the relationship was between cigarettes and a world shortage of grain we were never told.

The removal of the blackout screens did not make a great deal of difference until the dark nights returned. Then the yellow glow from paraffin lamps and candle light became not only friendly companions, but guardians that drove away all the ghosts and monsters that lurked in the darkness.

When the moon was bright the shadows of the men walking along the railway to and from the pit at Writhlington, would march across our bedroom wall making it possible to recognise the person to whom it belonged. Many times as we lay in our beds I told George who the person was, and despite the number of occasions when I called out to the person to prove it and received a "Wass thou want? You should be asleep this time of night, not hanging out the window shoutin' at I," in return, he remained unconvinced.

*   *   *

The feeling of euphoria following the end of the war had not, or so it seemed, affected just people. Now on clear mornings the smoke from the chimneys, as though released from the need not to give away our position to enemy bombers, rose up like fingers supporting dawn's pink sky. Sometimes, small clouds would move slowly toward it as if to warm their night-chilled fluffiness on the man-made heat.

Soon another kind of excitement made itself felt as the time for the return of the men and women who had fought in the war drew nearer. Welcome Home banners and flags began to appear, with each of the returning heroes being treated as if they alone had won the war. One was Sylv's father Bill.

Short of stature, it did nothing to diminish his happy out-look on life, or his strength in the support and defence of his family as one of the local farmers, a bad-tempered man, found out, soon after Mr Collin's return from the fighting.

Sylv and her brother Brian (Butch), were out playing in one of the fields when the farmer appeared and in his usual nasty manner ordered them out adding, "If I d'catch thee in here again, you'll get the weight of my stick down across your shoulders. Hurrying out of the field and indoors, they told their parents of the threat.

Off went Mr Collins down the hill and caught up with the farmer on the bridge over the brook. Several seconds later the farmer found himself hanging upside down over the bridge while Mr Collin's, holding him by the feet, assured him that the next time, if there was a next time, he'd put him over the bridge again and let go.

Funny how a few words of advice can change a person's outlook on life.

*   *   *

As the hours of daylight grew less and the nights began to draw in, a man named Mr Merryweather came to the village and started a weekly get-together called 'Sunshine Corner' in the Methodist church hall in Shoscombe. He was a tall, gangly man whose arms when he was speaking windmilled about in every direction. Initially, we didn't know what to make of him and went just to see what 'Sunshine Corner' was all about. After that first night I don't think we missed a single week. It was really good fun and we found him to be a very likeable and pleasant person.

*   *   *

During the war sweets and chocolate had not been high on the list of priorities deemed necessary to keep the country fed and clothed, so when the news went round that bars of chocolate could be bought at Filer's shop for sixpence the excitement was great. Though sixpence was a lot of money, the fact that each bar had sixteen small squares made them more than worth it.

After lunch I went to the bedroom and took six pennies from my money-box, wrapping them in my handkerchief to stop them clinking together; if mother had heard them, she would have made me put them back. At the end of afternoon lessons I went into Filer's and bought one of the bars which was called Ex-Lax.

Opening the wrapping paper I broke off one square and began sucking it slowly until it was gone. One was not enough and so I ate another. I had fully intended to share it with George and Ted but found before I knew it, that I had eaten the whole bar myself.

That evening severe stomach pains found me making hurried visits down the garden to the privy where, no sooner had I obtained relief than I had to begin all over again. It wasn't until I had been away for some time that mother came looking for me and found me almost unconscious, a result of eating the chocolate which had in fact been a laxative.

For over a week I was very ill, a victim of dehydration and greed. When I recovered I was punished for taking money from my box without asking permission and for the worry I had caused through my selfish actions. I often wondered what would have happened to me if I had been thoughtless enough to have died and added the cost of a funeral to their problems.

*   *   *

As life slowly began returning to normal people, for the first time in over six years, began making plans through the long dark nights of winter, the most important being where they would go for their summer holiday the following year. As we lived in the country, the obvious choice was the seaside.

Ilfey went with his parents and family to Lymington. While they were there the liners Queen Mary and Queen Elizabeth came into harbour for what was to be the last time, and the public were allowed onboard for conducted tours and to buy souvenirs.

Back at school after the holiday he brought with him two Biro pens, the first we had seen. What made them even more special was that each of them bore a picture of the liner they had come from.

Our holidays away from home was a day at Weston-super-Mare with the Sunday school, followed by another a few weeks later at Burnham with mother and Uncle Hube. The day at Weston was the most miserable I had ever known, the high point being when one of the girls stumbled while she was paddling and made a grab at another girl, causing them both to fall over and get soaking.

Burnham provided another day of high excitement. We went by train, which I enjoyed, stopping at every station on the way to let other children and their parents climb on. The zenith of that day was stopping at Binegar where the fruit-laden apple trees hung their branches over the platform begging to be picked. With most of the other children and many of the adults, we climbed out of the carriages and obliged.

Summer was no different from other seasons in the variety of weather it brought. On bright, heat-laden days, we would sit under the trees at the top of Greenstreet and look down on Shoscombe sunbathing in a sprawled out slump, while along the foot of the valley, Shoscombe Bottom shimmered under the heat haze and dreamed of dipping its feet into the cool clear water of the brook. On those days only the sounds of the countryside moved, creating background music to accompany Nature's summer overture

Most of the hot summer days we spent swimming at a bend in the brook behind Holdway's farm, where the movement of the water widening the banks had created quite a large pool. We were there one Sunday afternoon when the son of one of the local mine managers came along to the pool on the opposite bank. He was a boy who, because of his father's job, thought he was a cut above the rest of us; an attitude that had much to do with our dislike of him.

He stood for a while watching as we jumped in the water and splashed about before asking, "How do I get over there?"

"Come down the bank and wade across same as we do," we told him.

Taking off his shoes and socks he slid his way down the bank into the ankle deep water and began crossing. The snag was, after a few steps the bottom took a sudden plunge and you found yourself standing in water up to your chest.

Clambering out on our side looking very unhappy, he stood staring at us for quite a time before asking, "Why didn't you tell me it was so deep? Look at my clothes, they're soaking."

"Cos you didn't ask," Frank answered. "Anyroad, I dunt know how you got that wet. Our dog d'come across there regular and the water d'only come up to his belly."

Almost in tears, he took off his wet clothes and hung them over the bushes to dry. When we had finished swimming for the day we left him there a forlorn, but much less big-headed boy.

On another occasion when were swimming at Ten-foot, another boy arrived and began taking off his clothes.

"Wass reckon you'm gwanna do then?" we asked him.

"Swim," he told us.

"Swim! Thou cassent swim," Frank said.

"Course I can swim. I can swim as good as any of you. You watch me."

And with that he jumped in and promptly started to drown.

It was only because Ilfey, who was a good swimmer, was in the water at the time that saved chummy. Grabbing him, he brought him close enough for the rest of us to haul him out and lay him, gagging and retching, on the bank.

Often dark clouds would appear pressing the trapped heat into a clammy, sweat-filled weight, making breathing and any movement uncomfortable. On those days thunder, rumbling deep in its throat, would clamber heavily onto the backs of the sullen-faced clouds and ride their dark unfriendliness across the metallic blue of summer's sky.

Sometimes the grumbling would go on all day from behind the purple-tinged clouds until, as if it had been waiting for us to go to bed, the storm would begin, tearing the night sky open with shouts of anger. Then the rain, encouraged to even greater effort by the thunder's booming voice, and supported by sizzling slashes of lightning, would drive its slanting lances against the windows like mailed fists seeking entry into the comfortable safety of our homes.

* * *

I had gone to visit Auntie Weeks, something I did as often as possible, before going on to Frank's and back to Woodborough Pond to look for moorhens nests and collect some of the eggs to take home for eating. Many of the nests would have up to twenty eggs in them at the same time. One boy, so we had been told, had been out on the pond searching for nests when he caught a crab that overturned his boat. Must have been some size of crab we thought. A lot bigger than the ones we saw at the seaside or in Bob Swift's fish shop.

Reaching the pond we sat with the rough bark of one of the trees comforting our backs to eat the sandwiches Frank's mum had given us, before starting our search. A breeze sent ripples across the surface of the pond causing the ducks and other small water-fowl to bob about like pieces of coloured flotsam, while the swans large and aloof, sailed magestically on their way, not in the least

118

ruffled by the playfulness of the breeze.

On the far side of the pond a large, grey heron, eyes alert for its next meal, stilt-walked its way through the reeds until the sound of voices caused it to rise up and wing its way toward Codger's farm. As it disappeared two men came into the field leading six or seven pit ponies. Closing the gate, they took the halters off, and walked off the way they had come. The ponies, meanwhile, stood for a while not moving except for a nervous tossing of heads and pawing of the ground then, in a sudden burst of unleashed energy, they raced and pranced their way across the field, kicking up their heels to the accompaniment of whinnies of pure pleasure.

Above us the sun, boon to farmers and friend to children and pit ponies for the long, hot days it brought to their summer holiday, smiled its approval.

George, despite severe asthma attacks which caused him to miss many months of learning at school and his chance to sit the eleven plus exam still managed, despite grave doubts and strong opposition on the part of several of the teachers, to sit the entrance exam for Bath Technical College.

Soon after we had begun our summer holiday came the news of his success and with it an end to his schooldays at dear old St. Julian's. He was to take up his place in September when the schools and colleges reopened.

He had always been clever and quite well spoken, but his success made him even more conscious of speech and grammar to such an extent that he corrected in a helpful, but definitely not superior, way, anyone who spoke incorrectly in his presence. On one occasion involving Uncle Hube, however, good grammar was definitely relegated to second place.

We were sitting in the stable yard, the horse hitched up ready to go for a load of hay, when Uncle Hube arrived.

"Come on then," he said, "I'm gwanna learn thee how to use a hay knife."

Quick as a flash, George went in to action.

"Excuse me," he began, "It's not learn, it's teach. And you shouldn't say thee you should say y.."

Uncle Hube's large hand, landed with such force, that George was knocked off his feet and into the hedge, bringing an immediate end to his efforts to improve Uncle's grammar. Then putting his face down close to George's he said, "When I d'say learn thee, then I d'mean learn thee. I dunt need thee tellin' I how to speak. You baint one of they schoolteachers yet my son. Alright." Standing as though dumb George nodded. It didn't stop him correcting our grammar, he just made sure when he did it Uncle Hube was somewhere else.

George wasn't always on the receiving end. Sometimes it was he who handed out the thumps. He was a brilliant artist and was always doing drawings of animals, birds and people, and scenes from some of the films we saw, on any pieces of paper he could lay his hands on which he would then hide between the pages of his books, refusing to let anyone see them. This in no way stopped or deterred interested parties from taking and enjoying unofficial looks.

One day when he was out, I went through his books looking for any new drawings he may have done. Later that evening he came downstairs with one of those I'm-certainly-not-in-a-good-mood looks on his face.

"Someone's been at my books again," he announced, "And I want to know who?"

Generally, when he was wearing that look, I knew nothing about nothing, for to do so was to invite retribution to make a very painful visit to some part of your body. That day, for some reason, my thoughts became words before I had the chance to take them into custody, and with all the aplomb of the simpleton I was I blurted out "It was me."

The ensuing scuffle ended not only with him giving me a good thumping, but with mother supporting him with verbal asides like, "I've told you before to leave your brother's things alone," and "If I hear of you interfering with his things again, I'll send you to bed early for a week."

Some joke. If I was sent to bed early, who'd do my jobs?

Although it didn't stop me looking through his books, I still did so whenever the opportunity presented itself, I tried to make sure he never found out, and that my tongue never wagged at the wrong time again.

*   *   *

NINETEEN

1946. **Christmas,** slowing its journey to listen to the carols we sang, moved closer. The school party wrapped in the sandwiches, cakes and trifles we ate and tied with the games we played, brought us closer to the holiday.

Going home through a snow-covered landscape on the last day of term, we bowled snowballs ahead of us like marbles to see how big we could make them. At the top of the hill we started rolling one that by the time we had reached Mr Horler's house had grown so large we could hardly move it. Finally, just before the gateway into the stable yard, we had to give up.

That Christmas turned out to be the whitest for years as snow fell on snow until most of the country had been brought to a virtual standstill. We awoke one morning to snow so deep it reached halfway up our downstairs windows, through which we had to dig a path to reach and feed the hens, the horse and the pigeons. On the bridge at Ten-foot, icicles measuring several feet in diameter stood like glass pillars.

It was also the coldest winter on record for fifty-three years, and extended our holiday from two weeks to almost three months. No coal could be delivered, so we nailed a big box on the sledge and trekked to Braysdown for loads of wood chumps from the sawmill at the pit.

Another journey that had to be made every two days was to the top field to collect bags of hay for the stabled horse. As Uncle Hube had chosen that time to be ill, first with the flu and then with shingles, it was another job that fell to George and me.

Despite the weather many people still struggled to get to work. Chick Gregory, throughout those long, cold months, made his daily deliveries of milk using a sledge.

The weather also made it impossible for the children who were to sit the eleven-plus exam to reach the school. Only Glenda Collins and I managed to get there along with Mr White to supervise us.

Not that it made the slightest difference to any of us, in fact it did us a favour, for success would have meant having to go to Norton Grammar School, and none of us were interested in going to a school where the education included wearing a straw hat and carrying a hockey stick. Anyway, it would never have been as good as the education we received at St. Julian's.

*   *   *

Spring inevitably came, but muffled as it was beneath the snow, no-one noticed it. Spring flowers, snowdrops, daffodils and crocuses remained hidden, and even the trees and hedges seemed reluctant to allow their new buds and leaves out into such a cold, unfriendly world.

A sudden thaw that began in mid-March caused flooding, the like of which no-one in the area had experienced before, that added greatly to the loss of livestock and damage to property already caused by the long winter. After weeks of being submerged, it seemed almost impossible that the fields could recover in time to produce crops of any kind, but though more than a month later than usual, haymaking was done with no noticeable reduction in the size or quality of the crop.

Among the debris the floodwater left behind were some empty barrels, four of which we tied together to make a raft. Launching day arrived and we slid the raft down the bank into the brook and with a lot of slipping and sliding, managed to climb into the barrels and shove off from the bank to begin our expedition into the unknown.

It is a frightening experience escaping from an upturned barrel in the water. Once we were back on the safety of the bank the recriminations began. The ropes had not been tied properly. Someone must have got into the wrong barrel. Our balance had been wrong. All of which made not one jot of difference to the failure of the expedition as we sat, wet through and shivering, watching the water take our craft out of sight.

*   *   *

Every October the boys aged eleven years and over, were given a week off school to help on the farms gathering the potatoes, mangolds and swedes. Ilfey and I along with another boy, I don't remember who, got work on Small's farm at Stony Littleton.

We worked long, hard hours that week. Arriving at the farm while it was still dark, we would stand in the yard waiting for the tractor to bring the trailer that would take us to the field. Lunchtime, and it was back to the farm where, while the men sat down to a hot meal in the house, we sat in the barn eating our sandwiches washed down with the jug of cold milk that Mrs Small gave us.

Despite the hours of non-stop work we did it was the threat of reduced pay because we were not working hard enough that brought about the change in our attitudes. Another farm job was clearing the large stones from the fields, so

122

with the threat still ringing in our ears we decided that we would help with that while carrying on with the work of lifting the potatoes. During the next few days, for every five or six potatoes we picked up we also picked up two or three of the stones that we put into the sack beside them.

Farmer must have been pleased with us for on the Saturday evening before we left the farm for the last time, he came out and paid us our full wages of twenty-four shillings. That worked out at sixpence an hour.

*   *   *

Christmas and New Year, that seemed somehow to be far less exciting than those we had enjoyed during the war, came and went. As the weather became milder the cattle and horses were left out in the field again overnight.

Early morning each week-day, before the birds had ruffled the sleep from their feathers and begun calling good-morning to another day, before the breezes had begun to stir the hedges and gently shake the leaves awake, that was when the world belonged to Rustler and to me as we went to collect the horse.

One morning Prince, despite Rustler's growling at him to behave, was more fractious than I had ever known him to be. Added to the daily exercise of hopping about in order to keep clear of his teeth and hooves, every time I went near him with a piece of harness he moved and I had to start again. I managed to get him dressed eventually and backed into the cart. leaving only the tail stall to be put in position, a thing I never did in the stable but always while standing with one foot on the step of the cart and the other on the shaft; no way was I getting that close to his heels.

That day, everytime I got his tail bunched ready to pass through the loop, he swished it out of my hand. Losing my temper, I grabbed the brush we carried on the cart and jabbed him in the rump. Well, it was meant to be his rump, but with all his fidgeting around my aim was a little off so that instead of the intended target, I managed to poke most of the handle up his backside.

INSTANT ARMAGEDDON.

As his head went down, he kicked out his heels with such force that the boards in the bottom of the cart were sent flying in a storm of splintered missiles. Before the second kick landed I was off the cart and around the far end of the stable where I stood, wondering what to do next.

His screams of rage solved that problem as Uncle Hube came down the garden at a run. After he had managed to quieten him down, he unhitched him and led him back into the stable, staying with him until his rage subsided.

"Well there's one thing for sure," he said, coming out of the stable and looking at the damage done to the cart, "I wunt be makin' any deliveries 'til that bin fixed. What went and set'n off like that?"

"He've bin playin' up worse than usual all mornin',," I told him, which was the truth. "He kept jiggin' about all the time I was putting the harness on him then, when I got him in the cart, he went crazy." Which was also the truth.

I remained off school that day to help work on the cart. It took until late that evening to remove and replace all the damaged boards from the bed and sides of the cart. By that time we were both tired so that when he had finished screwing the name plate back on, he wrote his name and address on it in chalk saying, "I'll paint'n on later."

Several days later while he as was delivering a load of coal to a house at Green Parlour, one of the local constables noticed the name plate and drew Uncle Hube's attention to it.

"You bin at that job long enough to know you'm breakin' the law," he told him. "You d'know your name got to be painted on not written in chalk."

"I d'know that," Uncle Hube agreed, "But I were that tired when we finished t'other night that I did it in chalk 'til I had time to paint'n on."

"Well you should've found time afore you put the cart back on the road. I shall have to report thee."

The court, held in the Victoria Hall at Radstock, was full of Saturday night alcohol heroes, chalk users, and the general public when we arrived and sat down beside another coal haulier named Harry who, like Uncle Hube, had also been charged with a name plate offence.

Several cases were heard before a man sitting several rows in front of us was called. Standing up, looking big enough to get away with anything, he walked to the bench.

"You are charged with being on the premises of ....," the name of the pub was read out, "After business hours and with-out permission. You are also charged with resisting arrest and striking a constable several times.How do you plead?"

"Well 'twer his fault for interfering. He didn' have to come anywhere near. I'd of managed."

"Were you or were you not found on the premises named in the charge?" he was asked.

"Yes I were. You d'already know that."

"Would you explain what you were doing there?"

"I were tryin' to get out, weren't I?" he answered, to the great amusement of the listening people. "I went and fell asleep in there and when the landlord come round lockin' up, he must've missed seein' I. Well, I weren't gwanna bide in there all night were I? I wanted to get off home. Far's I'm concerned if thik bobby hadn' started layin' down the law, I would've and no harm done."

124

After a long sermon on taking too much to drink, he was given a stiff fine and ordered to keep away from the pub in question for six months.

Several more drunk and disorderlies were dealt with before Uncle Hube's name was called. Walking up to the bench, he stood while the charge was read out.

"Guilty, but ignorant of the law," he replied, when asked how he pleaded.

Following a lecture on the requirements of the law with regard to name plates on carts, he was ordered to put his name on the cart correctly and take it to the Red Post police station to show the constable it had been done.

When he returned to his seat, Harry leaned across and asked him, "What were thik word you said?"

"Ignorant. Plead guilty but ignorant of the law."

Harry's name was called and the charge read out. When he was asked how he pleaded Harry answered "Guilty", and was fined ten shillings with five shillings costs.

"Why didn' you say the same as I?" Uncle Hube asked him when we were outside.

"Cos when I got up there, I went and forgot thik darn word didn' I?" Harry explained.

*　　*　　*

Along with the week off school in October to help on the farms, all the boys, when we reached our eleventh birthday, moved from the short-trousered brigade and into long ones. This obvious sign of being 'grown-up' made us aware for the first time of our general appearance.

Haircuts especially, became of far greater importance for where, until then, most of us had been quite happy with the 'pudding-bowl' cut, that left us looking like Mo from the Three Stooges, we began to pay regular visits to Tom Gregory's barber shop at Peasedown where we sat with the other patrons, listening to the banter of men's talk.

Because of a disability in one of his legs, Tom had a seat fixed to the chair the customers sat in that enabled him to move around the person having their hair cut while sitting down. Late one summer afternoon, Frank took his place in the chair. Halfway through the cutting Tom stopped.

"I'm sorry young'un," he said, "I can't cut n'more today. You'll have to come back tomorrow and get'n finished."

"Wass mean, you can't cut n'more today?" Frank asked. "I can't go out home wi' only half me hair cut."

"You'm gwanna have to," Tom told him. "My leg's too bad for I to finish it now. He'll be better tomorrow. You come back then."

No amount of pleading on Frank's part could get Tom to change his mind. He just shoved him out of the shop and locked the door behind him.

When he arrived home, his mother saw the side of his head where the hair had been cut. When he turned after washing his hands she made, in Frank's words, a funny kind of sound and dropped the loaf of bread she was holding. "Wass up? Wass the matter?" he asked her.

"I dunt know," she said. "I reckon I must be startin' to see things. I were sure when you come in you'd had your hair cut."

"So I did. Well here anyroad," indicating his short bit of back and side. "I got t'go back tomorrow and get'n finished."

When he explained what had happened they both had a good laugh along with the rest of the family

"I'll tell thee I didn' half feel daft when he shoved I out that door and locked'n behind I," he told us later. "I went out home that fast I were just a blur; any quicker and they boots of mine would've caught fire. Didn' help I any wearin' thik balaclava either when I went back to get'n finished. The shop were full of back-shift miners when I got there, and you d'know what they'm like."

*   *   *

TWENTY

Although we were aware that girls were different to boys through the games we played, it almost cost me half a crown to learn they were not as uninteresting as they appeared when an outing to the Bath and West Show was arranged for the older pupils. I had been telling Uncle Hube about it when he had taken two half crowns from his pocket and handed them to me.

"There's something for thee to spend when you d'get there," he said. "Though if `twer I, I'd save one for another day."

Later, once my work was finished, I put one of them in the tin I used as a money-box then with the other in my pocket, I walked along the track toward Little Wood to be alone and plan the spending of my fortune. In days when a shilling was wealth, half a crown was a king's ransom.

I was sitting in the field when June, a girl to whose house we delivered coal and with whom I had become good friends, came along the track. Seeing me, she climbed through the fence and came across to where I was sitting.

"I were comin' to your house," she said, "I got to give a message to Mr Howell from my dad. Anyway what you doin' along here by yourself lookin' all serious?"

"I'm not serious," I told her. I'm thinkin' about the school trip to the Bath and West Show."

"Why, dunt you want to go?"

"Course I want to go. I'm just makin' plans for spending the half crown Uncle Hube gave me."

"He never gave you half a crown. You'm havin I on."

"I'm not," I assured her.

"Let's see it then."

I took the coin from my pocket and handed it to her adding at the same time, "He gave me two. The other one's along home in my tin."

She sat for a while turning the half crown over and over in her hand, then she said, "If you've got two you can let me keep this one seein' as how we'm friends. Then we'll have one each."

"And if you give it back to me then I shall still have two, wont I?" I told her, holding out my hand.

"What if I don't?" she queried, wrapping her fingers around it and hugging it close to her chest in the way girls do.

"Then I shall take it back," I assured her, grabbing her by the wrists.

Although she was a little older than me, and despite the fact that she had grown from the skinny girl she had been when I had first met her into the well-developed one she was then, she was still a girl. It would take me no time at all to retrieve my money.

Girl or not, she clung onto it like glue. It took me far longer, and a lot more effort than I had expected, due to all the wriggling and squirming she did. She proved to be as tricky as any of the boys I wrestled. Despite her resistance I eventually recovered it.

Once my money was safely back in my possession, I walked back to Radstock with her after she had delivered her message to Uncle Hube. I never mentioned our wrestling match to anyone in case it got back to mother, and it certainly wasn't something I wanted her to know about. Had some funny ideas about girls and boys did mother.

I don't think June said anything either for her mother was as nice to me as she had always been although her father, who remained as dislikeable as ever, did seem to look harder at me than usual although that may have been my imagination. He definitely did become more angry if he saw June talking to me. Several times I thought he was going to get physical. After that I stayed out of his way as much as I could.

His attitude made no difference to the liking June and I had for each other. As Radstock Market was a weekly focal point in the area, we regularly saw one another there on Saturday morning's. Soon after the recovery of my money, we began going to the pictures together in the afternoon. On the Sundays when she could make it, we would meet at Ten-foot in the afternoons and go for walks. Beat playing cricket into a cocked hat.

*　　*　　*

Another close but far less rewarding encounter, took place one evening after school. I came out of the house and found Sylv Collins playing two-ball against Jack Craddock's cow shed. I stood watching her for a while until one of the balls bounced near me. Catching it, I stood looking at her with a silly grin on my face.

"Let's have it back please," she said

"Suppose I don't?" I asked her.

"Then I'll clout you and take it back," she replied.

"Oh, ah!" I said, "And who's gwanna get to help thee?

"I wont need any help," she assured me. "Just let me have it back."

"You want'n, you come and get'n," I told her.

I never knew for sure if Sylv, for that brief moment, had forgotten that the war was over, or if there was another reason for her actions that day. Whatever it was, as she came up to me I stuck my chin out.

"Go on then," I said, "Let's see you clout me." So she did.

It was a dolly of a punch that caught me in the Adam's apple and dropped me, gasping and gagging for breath, on the road. Then, not in the least bit concerned about the purple colour my face had turned or the silent workings of my mouth as I tried to let her know I was dying, she began listing exactly what would happen if I was ever stupid enough to upset her again.

*　　*　　*

Jackdaws, if you got them young enough, made great pets and several of the boys had one. The best time to get them was just before they were ready to leave the nest, and the best place to get one in our area was from a nest in one of the hollow trees at the foot of Sileton's below the spinney.

It was almost impossible to get at the nests by climbing up the outside of the tree; to have any real chance of success you had to wriggle through a hole in the tree close to the ground and climb up inside. That is what Ilfey did the day he went to get his jackdaw.

With the bird safely in his shirt he climbed back down to find when he reached the foot of the tree, he couldn't get out. That left him with two choices. One was to let one of us hold the jackdaw for him, or two, he could keep hold of it and risk it escaping as he wriggled out.

He chose the second way "Cos if I d'give'n to one of you to hold, you'll keep'n," and after a great deal of ooching and ouching he emerged smiling, to the cawing support of his new pet.

*　　*　　*

During the summer holiday a troop of the Boy's Brigade came down from London and set up their tents in the field in front of the Rectory and Red Indians they were not. Their initial greeting to us was "Blimey mate, dun arf stink abaht 'ere dunnit?"

It wasn't long though before we had all made ourselves known to one another, and after a few days they joined in many of the things we did. Several of them who were interested, went with us one day to experience ferreting. We began their instruction by letting them carry the ferrets in their boxes and the heavy bag of nets. It turned out to be a good day and in less than two hours we had a dozen rabbits, which we left lying to gut later.

129

One of the boys became so excited he decided to give us his impression of one of the hunters we saw in the westerns at the pictures. Picking up one of the rabbits he put it on his head and began dancing about whooping and wailing in a way that sounded more like someone with a very bad toothache than a hunter

What he didn't know was that the rabbit was still full of water which was forced out to run wetly through his hair and onto his clothes. The strongly-scented impression it left, ensured that he did not share the closeness of the group on our way home.

*   *   *

The back door of Frank's 'castle' led directly into the pit yard, the place where many of the things we did began. To the left of the sawmill, the track led to the pit pond where we collected most of our frog-spawn in jam jars, which we sat in our bedroom windows while we waited for the black specks to become tadpoles.

To the right was the pit-head which had a sloping ramp, like those at the end of station platforms, leading up to the working area. At the top of the ramp was the 'tally' room, the most important single feature above ground at all the pits in the area.

On the wall outside hung the 'tally' board, on which the miners, before going below ground, hung a round, brass disk, called a tally, that gave an instant knowledge of the number of men below at any time of the day or night. At the end of their shift, the miners would take their tally from the board and put it in a box in the tally room.

Outside the tally room at Braysdown stood a large drum of carbide from which the miners filled their tins at the start of each shift to provide the light they needed to work. It was also much in demand by us, for used in an enclosed space such as a lemonade bottle with a screw top, it made a very powerful and destructive weapon, ideal for blowing things up.

It was that drum of carbide that led to Frank becoming the youngest and most reluctant miner in Somerset, probably in all of Britain, since Lord Shaftesbury had been successful in stopping women and young children being employed underground and in factories.

It was usually on a Sunday when the pit was less busy that we 'obtained' our carbide, and on the Sunday in question it was Frank's turn to get it. When we arrived there were several surface men at work loading timber onto the top of the cage before sending it below to be used as roof supports.

Waiting until they had gone into the tally room for their break, he crept up the ramp and crouching beside the drum he scooped up a tinful. Until then, things had gone as they had on the previous occasions. That day, however, just as

Frank turned away, Joby Carey came out onto the plates and saw him.

Grabbing him by the arm he asked, "Wass reckon you'm doin' here then?"

"Nothin'," Frank answered him. "I 'ent doin' nothin'."

"You lyin' little toad. Wass that you've got there?" said Joby, pointing at the tin Frank was holding. "You'm here to pinch carbide. Well you bin and come to the wrong place. Now I'm gwanna show thee what d'happen to they what can't keep their fingers out of other people's drums of carbide. Then you wunt be s'quick t'do it again."

There was only one sort of lessons taught for such things and we could almost feel the pain before the first blow landed. Imagine then our shocked surprise when Joby, helped by Gilb Andrews, put Frank on top of the cage, pulled the chain tightly around him and rapped the ready-to-lower signal to the winding engine driver.

How he felt as the cage began its descent, none of us had any idea. Terror! Horror! Disbelief! They were only a few of the emotions we felt as we saw him disappear, certain that we would never see him again. The most worrying thing of all was how were we going to tell Mrs Weston and who was going to do it. It was something that required a great deal of thought, for when she heard her umbrella was sure to come into play.

The decision was made for us when Frank, riding this time inside the cage, made his return. Gathering in a huddle by the pond he told us what had happened.

The shaft at Braysdown had a bend in it and as the cage rocked about on the guides Frank, looking up, saw the ring of light above him getting smaller and smaller until, with a kind of shuddering movement, the cage went through the bend and the light disappeared. Another feature of the shaft was the constant fall of water from its sides, so that by the time the cage reached pit bottom Frank was not only very relieved but also very wet.

"Wass reckon you'm doin' on top that cage then?" asked the very surprised bottom banksman. "You'm not supposed to be up there."

"I d'know that," Frank told him. "I didn' ask t'be here. I didn' want t'come down. Twer they up top what sent I."

"Well you must've bin up to summat for'm t'do that. They wouldn' send thee down here for nothin'."

He lifted Frank down and sat him out of the way until the other men had unloaded the timber. Then putting him inside the cage, they sent him back to the surface.

The challenge and excitement of getting carbide deserted us for a while after that, but with the healing process of short memories we soon returned to the carbide drum, albeit with a far greater vigilance.

We were digging a cave in the side of the batch one day when the whole thing collapsed burying Ivan Chivers.

"Ivan bin and got hisself buried," someone called out.

"Best place for'n," came the answer. "Let'n bide there."

"We can't do that," said Jack Weston.

"Why not?" we asked him.

"Cos we d'need'n to make up sides for a game of cricket, thass why not," Jack told us.

So we dug him out.

*　　*　　*

Only grown-ups called it stealing. They never seemed to understand how the rich reds and bright yellows of the apples could take away all reason until there was no right or wrong, only desire.

Frank, Barry White, Joe Fussell and Tony Ford becoming victims of that desire, found themselves filling pockets and stomachs from the trees in Gullick's orchard, although they could be bought six for a penny at the farmhouse or got for nothing from our own trees. It was the sound of Mrs Gullick's voice asking "Whose that up in my trees?" that brought them back to the reality.

Spurred into action they dropped from the trees like the ripe fruit they were so busily eating and took off round the farmhouse, where they ran straight into Mrs Gullick coming out the back door. Heads bowed, they stood silently in front of her.

"Right," she said, "Which one of thee were it up my trees takin' my apples?"

No-one answered.

"Wunt do any good just standin' there lookin' as if you be all daft and dunt know what I be on about."

Still no answer.

"Well if none of thee is gwanna tell I, then I'll tell you. Twer he wass got the red nose."

Immediately four hands went up and four noses received a brisk rub. As they did so, their owners realised what they had done.

Luck was with them for all they received was a lecture from Mrs Gullick and sent on their way. She even allowed them to keep the apples they had scrumped.

*　　*　　*

Not everyone unfortunate enough to get caught was that lucky, such as the time George and I were so bewitched by the deep, shiny redness, of the apples on the tree at the back of Gullick's farmhouse we just had to have some. Throwing large sticks, we brought the apples down like red hailstones and had

132

almost filled our shirts when Joe Gullick came hurtling round the corner of the house with a look on his face that said just one thing...*RUN*. So I did. The strange thing was that although George never moved, Joe charged straight past him as though he wasn't there and followed my fast moving body along the track.

There was a five-barred gate at the far end that I never touched. I simply sailed over it and charged on across the field while taking the apples from my shirt and spraying them left and right in a modern day version of Johnny Appleseed, over the stile on the other side of the field, down the next field to a gap in the hedge and into our house where I collapsed in a breathless heap.

That was my second mistake of the day for the scullery door burst open behind me and into the house came Joe. Before I could move, or mother could speak, he was knocking the tar out of me.

When he'd had enough he thumped me down on the settle and began telling mother the reason for his visit. As he spoke, I could see by the look on her face that she was even less pleased with me than Joe was. When he had gone she added more bruises to the one's Joe had given me, and sent me to bed without tea or supper.

George's part in the affair was never mentioned and we often wondered afterward if Joe, in his apparent desire to catch me, had run past George without seeing him.

The worst thing about the entire episode was not the hidings or being sent to my room, but the apples themselves. It turned out they were cider apples. I wouldn't have been able to eat them had I got safely away.

*　　*　　*

Apples were not the only magnets that attracted the filings called children to them, other kinds of fruit were equally as guilty. One, a greengage tree that produced the largest fruit in the area, grew in one of the neighbouring villages and led three of us to walk over there one afternoon to relieve it of some of its burden.

We hadn't been up the tree long, when a man appeared and stood looking up at us.

"You look as if you're enjoying yourselves," he said.

"You'm right there," we assured him. "They be lovely. You want some?"

"Not just now," he answered walking away, to return a few minutes later with an older man who asked us what we thought we were doing.

"Pickin' fruit for the farmer," we told him, "Why?"

"Why? 'cos I d'own this orchard and I never asked you t'pick my fruit. If you'm not down that tree in ten seconds, I'll send for the Bobby to help thee."

The word 'Bobby' was our fast ladder to the ground, where a dozen or more of the village men were standing around watching what was going on.

"Where d'you lot come from then? I haven't seen any of you around here afore," the owner asked.

"Over Radstock way," we told him.

"You've had a tidy walk to get here then."

One of the men, there's always one isn't there? asked, "Want I t'go and fetch the bobby?"

"No. I got a better idea," the owner told him. "Seein' as how they've come all the way over here to pick greengages, thass what I'm gwanna let them do. Course," he went on, giving us a hard look as he spoke, "if they dunt want to, then you can go and get the policeman down here. Now you lot get on along home and bring back your fruit baskets; we'm gwanna let these visitin' harvesters fill'm for thee."

Of all the punishments we could have received, that was the worst. We spent the rest of the afternoon and evening picking fruit until we had cleared not only the greengage tree, but several apple trees as well, and each time we handed down a full basket to the owner everyone clapped and cheered. It was an act that added greatly to the embarrassment of being caught taking something that didn't belong to us without the owner's permission.

*   *   *

TWENTY-ONE

Depending on whether you were an adult or a child, nineteen forty-nine brought some startling and traumatic changes to most of our lives. To the adults fell the choice of having, or not having, electric lighting brought into their homes. No pressure was put on any of them to accept, but those who did were given several options.

They could have it put in just one room or throughout the house. Those deciding to have it in four rooms, would have it put in the fifth room free. It seemed a very good offer until you realised that most of the houses only had four rooms or less. While most households decided for it there were those, Uncle Hube among them, who did not regard it as a good thing, due to what they believed were the hidden dangers involved.

"Where do it go when you can't see it?" they asked. "What if it d'build up and explode while we'm in our bed? Be worse than a thunderbolt hittin' thee. Wouldn' do us a lot of good if we all finished up sleepin' down the stable wi' the hoss, would it?"

*   *   *

As far as we children were concerned, our trauma began just before the new school year commenced. We had begun our summer holiday that year not knowing that each one of us aged eleven years and over, was leaving our much-loved school for the very last time. That never again would we know the joy of being one of its pupils, or the friendship and family closeness of our schoolfriends and teachers.

The holiday was almost over before we found out that a way of life was ending, had ended, courtesy of legislation by Central Government, based on the 'findings' of another of one of their committees who always 'know' what's best. Findings that gave no thought to the effect it would have on communities such as ours.

Neither did they seem to care that it would lead them eventually to lose much of their identity, individuality and the feeling of belonging, as they became submerged beneath the weight of a totally uncaring and blind bureaucracy.

*   *   *

The new school year arriving bright and shiny, did little to cheer us as we waited at the Red Post for the bus that would deliver us to Radstock where the Board School, our new educational establishment awaited our arrival. It was a school that was to leave many of us lasting memories.

There were the children, many of whom we already knew from going to the pictures and the market, who did their best to make us feel welcome, while others did nothing to hide the fact that they didn't like us. There were the teachers, all of who seemed to be devoid of any of the caring friendliness we had always been used to, and finally the school itself. Whoever had thought of building it in the first place together with whoever had chosen the site on which it was built, had left behind them the firm statement that they did not like children.

Standing at the top of a steep hill, its cold and aloof unfriendliness was reflected throughout its classrooms; none of the warmth we had always known at St. Julian's had managed to sneak through the doors of that building. Its playground, clinging desperately to the steeply sloping side of the hill, made games, especially ball games, impossible to play with any real enjoyment.

It was at that school that several of us became aware of the fear charged, stomach tightening excitement, of playing truant. Fields and woods, ponds and batches, hedges and lanes all became custodians of our rebellion. Cloud shadows, racing each other and us across the freedom of the fields, became our silent conspirators.

The days on which we were absent most often were chosen in order to miss woodwork. We had been doing the subject for several years before we went to Radstock under a teacher named Mr Sparks who was, without doubt, the toughest teacher we ever had. At Radstock the master, instead of extending the skills we had already acquired, made some of us go back to the beginning and start all over again. A decision guaranteed to relegate him to the position of least liked and respected of our teachers.

We also had to choose the days we 'skipped' school with great care, for detection would have meant a long-lasting and very painful retribution. Also, to be caught on several or more occasions could well have resulted in us being sent to a school where the education would have been 'approved'.

As the year moved into the colder weather, so it became more easy to find suitable excuses. Colds were worth three days absence, while the flu was worth at least a week and sometimes longer

The neglect of our education could not continue undetected for ever and it didn't. As soon as she found out mother took me away from the school, and more importantly away from my friends, and sent me, together with my brother Ted, to school in Bath.

It was a decision that did nothing to lessen the number of days I 'missed' school. On the contrary, it increased them.

Thankfully we were only there until Easter, before mother changed our school again, this time to Downside. Not the college but St. Benedict's, one of the two village schools that sheltered beneath the high walls of the abbey, where under the influence of Sister Angela and Mr Wills, I began to enjoy school again.

Refelecting as it did much of the attitude of our school at Shoscombe, it brought to an end all my acts of truancy. It's strange how different environments and attitudes have such a good or bad effect on people, especially children.

*   *   *

Reaching Gaston's end of the footpath on my way to the mill at Radstock one Saturday morning, I found Frank sitting on the fence beside Little Wood with a face on him that made him look about as happy as a mud wall. No smile. No greeting. Not at all his usual cheery self.

"Where's thou gwine then?" he asked, the tone of his voice saying he wasn't in the slightest bit interested.

"The mill for corn," I told him. "You comin'?"

"Not today I'm not," he answered, "I dunt feel too good."

"I thought by that look you got on your face that there were somethin' up. Wass the matter with thee?"

"Snakes," he said, thass what's the matter wi' me. I were up that spinney above Cleeve and went and sat down on an adder didn' I?" He gave a huge shudder. "I'll tell thee, I d'hate they bloomin' things."

"Did it bite thee?" I asked him.

"No it didn'. I didn' sit there long enough for'n to bite I. He made I jump though. I went that high I could see the top of Wellow church."

Although I sympathised with him, I couldn't help laughing at what he said. Still chuckling I carried on to the mill while he, climbing down off the fence, hunched his way back up the hill toward Braysdown and home.

*   *   *

There are times when something happens for which there seems to be no logical explanation. Such an event occurred one night involving the woman who had moved into our cottage shortly after we had moved into Uncle Hube's house.

We were eating our supper when the parlour door opened and the woman staggered in looking very ill and in a state of collapse. Going to her quickly, mother took her arm and sat her down.

"What on earth is the matter?" she asked.

"It's my Bob," the woman whispered. "He's been killed at work."

"Oh, my goodness," mother gasped. "Who came to tell you?"

"No-one came to tell me. I saw him," she said, and burst into tears.

Several cups of tea later she told us the strangest story we had ever heard. This is what she said.

"I had gone upstairs to bed and was sitting on the chair taking off my shoes, when he suddenly came out of the corner by the window, walked over to me and said 'Everything's going to be alright', then walked across the room and disappeared through the wall into Mrs Wallace's cottage. That's when I knew."

We looked at her as if she had gone mad. How could such a thing happen. She must have been dreaming.

Several hours later a man from the pit and a policeman took that idea from our heads, when they arrived to confirm what she had told us.

Some months after the event, when she had recovered from the shock, we asked her how she had known what had happened before the men had arrived to tell her.

"Because I've got second sight," she told us.

"Second sight?" we asked, mystified. "What does that mean?"

"It means I can sometimes see things that have happened before anyone tells me, or things that are going to happen before they do."

"But how do you get second sight?" we wanted to know.

"Have you ever heard of the seventh child of the seventh child? No. Well that's what I am, and because of that I've got second sight."

We were never really sure what to make of her explanation and we discussed it many times afterwards. One thing we were sure of was the fact that on that night she had known what had happened before she'd been given the news officially.

That, sadly, was not the only pit fatality that year. Another miner at Haydn who had been off work through illness for three weeks, was killed on the day he returned when one of the ponies bolted.

On the brighter side, Yeovil Town's surprise defeat of Sunderland in the F.A. Cup caused great local interest. Their team captain and manager was Alec Stock from Peasedown, who was married to Marge Filer whose father ran the store and Post Office opposite the school.

That shock result gave many of the locals the chance to recall, true or otherwise, other events and happenings they had experienced. The stories came that fast and thick it was impossible to tell which were true and which leg-pullers. The one I liked the best was a story about a mushroom.

"I remember," said the storyteller, "one morning I were gwine up across the fields when I came across the biggest mushroom I've ever seen. I'll tell thee,

138

he were that big I had to drive three sheep out from under'n afore I could cut'n down."

*   *   *

Added to the scarcely controlled excitement the annual trips to the seaside brought, were the madly exciting journeys I was forced to make once a fortnight with mother to Bath, and though I truly loved the train travel, it did nothing to ease the depression those days brought me. I hated them.

Though George, who always enjoyed going and volunteered to go in my place, mother wouldn't hear of it. When it was my turn to go I went, and Lord help me if I didn't enjoy every second.

The trips for me ended the day I nearly caused mother's death. As we were approaching the platform at Single Hill on the way home, she told me to wait until she was off the train so that we could cross the line together. However, by the time the train had stopped I had forgotten her instructions and ran off along the platform with her chasing after me.

I made it safely across to the other side, but as she came from behind our train, a goods train coming from Radstock thundered into the station. It was the quick thinking of Renee Tapper the Station Mistress that saved her, for seeing there was no way she was going to get across in time she screamed at her to "Get under the platform." Mother only just made it for as the train rushed past, it cut the bottom of her coat off.

She emerged shaken, and bleeding from a cut on her head where she had knocked it against the concrete of the platform as she dived under it. I think everyone there that day warmed their hands on some part of my body. In addition to the physical pain, was the 'pain' of having my trips to Bath stopped, not for just a limited period, but forever. Life can sometimes be terribly unfair.

*   *   *

139

TWENTY-TWO

It **always seemed to me** that in January, once the New Year was over, Winter's chilling grip began to loosen as the days slowly began to lengthen and move steadily toward Spring.

Though it gave us little to applaud as being in any way gentler or kinder than December's, January's weather, despite the frosts that still whitened the land and kept the drinking troughs and ponds ice-capped, despite the rains driven still by wintry winds, despite the need to wrap up warmly before going out, always seemed less cold, less unfriendly.

I especially liked the foggy mornings when on my way to Frank's, I would stop at the top of Greenstreet and look down on Shoscombe where only the chimneys of the cottages could be seen poking above the grey mantle. From them smoke, almost the same colour as the fog, spiralled upward as though the fires had pulled the greyness into the cottages and released it again through their chimneys. As I watched, other chimneys would begin advertising the fires newly lit in their hearths to the accompanying sounds of doors opening and closing and voices, muffled by the fog, as their owners made their way to the privies to carry out the all important morning offices.

Despite the weather, the work of delivering the miners coal went on. Every load for Peasedown had to be hauled up Gaston's Hill which, because of its steepness, required us to stop under the bridge at Ten-foot and put a climbing nail in each of the horse's front shoes.

One morning I had just begun putting the nails in when a car coming down past the pit was forced to stop due to the narrowness of the road. The driver waited for a while before giving a blast on his horn causing Prince to jump and knock me over.

Quietening him down, Uncle Hube picked up the hoof and finished putting the nail in before doing the same with the other one, during which time the driver of the car sounded his horn again several times. Finally, exasperated at being held up, he got out of the car.

"You going to be there all day?" he asked angrily.

Uncle Hube slowly picked up the tools and put them away in the tool box on the cart, then checked the harness and the chains before turning to the man.

"I dunt know," he told him. "I might be."

"Well d'you think that you could get a move on?" the man snapped at him.

"I could, but I wunt. I'm gwanna make sure the hoss is how he should be afore I d'move."

"Well get a move on anyway. I can't wait here all day."

"Sounds to I as if you'm in a bit of a hurry," said Uncle Hube. "I get the feelin' wi' all the shoutin' you'm doin' and the noise you'm makin' wi' that car horn, that you d'fancy you'm a pretty important somebody. Well you'm gwanna have to learn a bit o' patience. I baint about to go any quicker just cos you be in a hurry."

"Course I'm in a hurry," the man said angrily, "And you're holding me up. I happen to be a councillor and I'm on my way to a meeting."

"A councillor, and in a hurry too," said Uncle Hube. "I dunt think I've met one o' they afore. In that case we'd both better get movin' else you wunt get to that meeting and I wunt earn any coin."

With that he took Prince's bridle and began leading him up the hill in such a way that denied the car the room to pass until we reached the track along to Cleeve where all the hauliers stopped to give the horses a breather. As we led Prince off the road, the car went past us with another angry blast of its horn.

"Were you not worried about him?" I asked, as we watched the car disappear at the top of the hill.

"You reckon he had somethin' about'n to worry I?" he asked me.

"Well he's a councillor," I told him. "I thought when he told you that you'd move out of his way."

"Ah, so did he my son, so did he. But you listen to what I'm gwanna tell thee. You'm gwanna meet a lot like he in your life. People what d'run about as if they d'own everything in sight, and tellin' everybody how important they be. But tidn't the person what's important 'tis the job and how well 'tis done. As for he wass just gone on up the hill well, I dunt reckon he's any more important today than he were yesterday."

*   *   *

I was given my first adult bicycle by an old lady who lived at Westfield. Because of her age we always put the coal into the coal house for her, for which she always rewarded us with a cup of tea. We were sitting on the low garden wall one day drinking our tea when she asked me if I had a bike.

"No," I told her. "But I can always borrow one if I need to."

"There's one up the garden in the shed that belonged to my husband that you can have if you d'want it. You go on up and have a look at'n."

I found, when I took it out of the shed, that it had only a front wheel, but that posed no problem at all as I carried it down the garden and put it into the cart. A brand new one couldn't have made me more happy.

When I got it home Mr Gray gave me a back wheel that caused a few smiles, as the wheel on the bike was a twenty-six inch while the one he gave me was a twenty-eight.

"That'll cut down the wind and help thee go faster," he told me, as he fixed the wheel into the frame.

Having a bike allowed me to do some of my jobs, such as going to the mill, more quickly, giving me more time to do the things I wanted to. I fixed a box on the carrier above the back mudguard in which Rustler sat. We travelled scores of miles together on that bike and enjoyed every one of them.

* * *

In March a shot-firing accident at New Rock that killed one man and left another seriously injured, made us aware yet again that the real price of coal could never be measured by how much the greedy coal-owners could get for it, but by the deaths and injuries suffered by the men who spent all their working lives in the suffocating blackness and danger of the pits harvesting the crop, while above ground wives and mothers waited.

The late Frank Marsh, who lived and worked at Braysdown, recounted to us an incident that had taken place underground involving one of the pit ponies. Apparently it had left its stall and gone wandering about, only to end up down the sump. When the men turned up for work the next day, some hours were lost removing the dead animal before the shaft could be used.

Once it had been done the men responsible for the ponies, Frank among them, went to the owner's office to report what had happened.

"He weren't too pleased when we told'n," Frank told us. "He shouted and

142

cussed as if we were to blame. He made it sound as though we'd taken thik pony out the stall and pushed'n down the sump. And wass think he said when he'd stopped all his cussin' and bawlin'? He said, "Do you lot know how much its going to cost me to replace that pony? Two pounds ten shillings, that's how much. Pity that hadn't been a man that went down the sump, I could've got another one of they for free."

* * *

April the fifteenth saw the closure of Camerton Colliery for economic reasons, with the men being deployed to other pits in the area. The closure not only affected the families of the miners concerned, but also the families of the men who worked on that stretch of the railway.

The busy line, already closed to passenger service, which had carried countless tons of coal from the pits at Camerton and Dunkerton, closed some years earlier, almost overnight became a relic. Where until then trains had run fairly regularly throughout the day, now several weeks elapsed between the departure of one and the arrival of the next.

* * *

May was almost over when a death that shocked us all, that of Les Gray, occurred. He had gone out for the evening with a friend and on the way home the motorcycle they were riding touched the kerb coming down Wells Hill in Radstock. Both men were thrown off and Les, who was only thirty-two, died of his injuries. What a tragic irony it seemed that he should have survived fighting in the war, only to die in the peace of the Somerset countryside.

* * *

In the years following the end of the war a tramp began appearing in the village, usually at haymaking and harvesting time. We would look up from our work and there he would be, standing on the cinder path watching us.

One of the men would walk down the field with a bottle of cold tea and some sandwiches, which the tramp would put into his overcoat pocket before going off along the path. The next morning without fail, the empty bottle would be lying against the rick when we arrived at the field.

In September a man was charged with stealing one and a half hundred weight of coal from the batch at Writhlington, valued at four shillings and sixpence. He had been collecting the bits of coal that were mixed in with the waste material sent up from underground, when the manager saw him and sent for the police.

"I dunt know what all the fuss and bother is about," the man said in answer to the charge. "All I did were pick up the bits of coal what bin lyin' about the batch for years. How can you accuse someone of stealin' somethin' wass bin thrown away? If its bin thrown away that d'mean the owner dunt want it anymore. But if he dunt want it, that dunt mean t'say no-one else do. They bits of coal bin lyin' on that batch since before the Coal Board took the pits over. Even before some on us were born."

He was fined ten shillings.

*   *   *

Autumn returned bringing with it the smell of well-ripened apples, picked and stored before the first of the frosts laid cold, damaging fingers on them. Smoke from the bonfires rose like prayers, carrying with it all our hopes for as short and gentle a winter as possible.

October sneaked in again and fog, that wriggled its way through our clothing making us damply cold for the rest of the day, accompanied us most mornings as we set off for one of the farms to lift potatoes and twist mangolds out of the frost-hard, unforgiving earth.

That week, despite all the other work we did throughout the year, remained still the hardest and most tiring of all.

With bonfire night rapidly approaching, most of our spare time was spent collecting as much material as possible. Old car and tractor tyres, broken and no longer wanted pieces of furniture, branches that had fallen, or been helped to fall, from the trees, were all built up into a huge pile. On the top of it all we put an old chair on which, like an old-time monarch, the guy sat, waiting for the special night when all of his subjects would gather to pay him homage.

Our bonfire building one year was constantly hindered by one of the pullets that had somehow acquired a talent for escaping that would have been appreciated by prisoners of all kinds. She must have been related to Houdini, for despite all we did to stop her, she kept getting out of the run where even the closest inspection showed no breaks or holes either in the fence or in the house.

At first she was easily caught with a handful of corn, but as her escapades continued it began to grow more difficult. On one occasion, after dodging her squawking way around the garden with us in pursuit, she took refuge in a large bed of stinging nettles that grew in a corner of the garden to attract butterflies.

"You'll catch her now easy enough if you'm quick," said Mr Horler, who was looking over his hedge watching our antics.

Recalling a previous encounter I'd had with nettles, quick was one thing I had no intention of being, as we stood looking at the nettles slyly nodding their heads in the breeze, as though inviting unsuspecting fingers to 'come and touch us'.

Uncle Hube, pushing his way into the nettles caught her and at the same time showed us how to stop her escaping permanently. Generally, we had chicken only at Christmas and Easter. That year we had it in November as well.

Those of us whose family fortunes did not extend to buying fireworks, were invited into the garden of someone whose did. Johnny (Nipper) Dyson always gave us an invite. However, Doug and Frank Wallace, determined that we should have some of our own, made several using as their starting point twelve-bore cartridges from which the pellets had been removed.

Bonfire night came and the festivities were well under way when we gathered to let off the home-made bangers and boy, were they good. They blew the window out of the workshop, damaged the door, completely demolished several fruit bushes and left a hole in the garden that we reckoned was as deep, if not deeper, than the one made by the land-mine in the field at Ten-foot, in ninteen forty-one.

"Another half a foot and I reckon we'd be able to see the miners lamps down underground," Mr Horler commented to Uncle Hube, as they stood surveying the scene next morning.

*   *   *

TWENTY-THREE

Easter **1951 signalled an end** to the days of uncluttered infancy and childhood that until then we had enjoyed. Beyond the day of leaving school the days of work beckoned, when we would each attend our places of employ.

Frank to Candy's farm at Foxcote, Ilfey to the butcher's department at Peasedown Co-op, where Audrey Blacker was already working as a counter assistant in the provisions department, while Sylv Collins went first to Dent's glove factory along Waterloo Road in Radstock, then to Clarke's shoe factory at Westfield.

Herksy and I went to the pits, he to Norton Hill and me to Writhlington, where I joined many of the men I had been privileged to grow up among, and rode with them down into the dark confines of the mine where, hopefully, I too would start to become a man.

*   *   *